MW01036470

From Knocking on Doors to Making Millions

Top Strategies for Direct Sales Success

Tamika,

To Your

You are braver than you believe
Stronger than you seem
Smarter than you think
And loved more than you know

Success!!

Elizabeth Demas

Elizabeth Demas

Copyright © 2016 by Elizabeth Demas

All rights reserved. This book or any portion thereof may not be reproduced or used in any manner whatsoever without the express written permission of the publisher except for the use of brief quotations in a book review or scholarly journal.

This publication is designed to provide general information in regard to the subject matter covered. However, laws and practices often vary from state to state and are subject to change. Because each factual situation is different, specific advice should be tailored to the particular circumstances. For this reason, the reader is advised to consult with his or her own advisor regarding their specific situation.

The author has taken reasonable precautions in the preparation of this book and believes the facts presented in the book are accurate as of the date it was written. However, neither the author nor publisher specifically disclaim any liability resulting from the use or application of the information contained in this book. The information is not intended to serve as a legal, financial, or other professional advice related to individual situations.

It is sold with the understanding that the author is not engaged in rendering legal, accounting, or other professional services. If legal or other professional assistance is required, the services of a competent professional person should be sought.

First Printing: 2016

ISBN: 978-1-5304-7693-0

Edited by: Emily Garry

Published by: Clarity Path Consulting, LLC
www.claritypathconsulting.com

Book available in print, digital, and (soon) audible versions.

Elizabeth is recognized as a national leader and business person by Avon, with her original store selling more than any other of the privately held Avon stores in the US. Elizabeth uses systems and processes to orchestrate her well run store, teaching her employees the importance of success measures and financials. Elizabeth is known by her peers as a giving, smart business person they can turn to when their business seems challenging. I look forward to what the future holds for Elizabeth, a future she continues to design, reaching her goals and ambitions.

Sally Smith
Smith & Associates, Inc.
www.mindseries.com

To say that Elizabeth with an MBA, high energy level, and Go Giver spirit is a positive force in the Avon retail world would be an understatement. She owns and operates one of the most successful Avon Stores in the country and she achieved that tremendous success in record time. Authentic and completely transparent, Elizabeth shares from the heart and contributes daily to the success of many of her peers. It should come as no surprise to anyone who knows her that she has written a book. It was the logical next step for Elizabeth who is a teacher at heart.

Pat Puzder
Avon Store owner
2012 Avon Woman of Enterprise

Elizabeth is fantastic! She is very knowledgeable and well read. She also has the ability to explain ideas in simple, practical ways. She is tireless in her effort to find ways of succeeding.

Denise Lewis
Avon Store owner

Once in a while, you are blessed to meet and know someone who has a natural gift for business. Elizabeth is down to earth and very business savvy. I have had the pleasure to watch her retail operations continue to grow even when the economy is shaky. She gets it and knows how business works.

Steve Waddell
I Support Learning
www.ctelearning.com

Elizabeth is an excellent retailer. She came into our location and in five minutes told us how to rearrange things so we would sell more. We did it and every person that has come into the store has purchased add-ons that they normally would not have. Success in less than a week. Can't beat that!

Connie Hernandez
ReUse Concrete Sealing Specialists, LLC
sealgreen.com

Elizabeth, thank you for the information you have shared. Using your insight and knowledge has increased my business and decreased my paperwork. You have a gift – good luck and thanks.

Peggy Roberts
Avon Store owner

Elizabeth serves as an inspiration to those who are paying attention.

Tim Schaefer
Principal at Tim Schaefer & Associates LLC

I find people don't always understand the considerable investment in time and effort that is needed to succeed. This issue is one of many areas that are covered very well in your book. The lessons in the book go beyond any particular product line.

Deborah Burkley
Professor of Business Administration
Southwest Minnesota State University

Elizabeth has been very helpful to us in organizing our Licensed Avon Beauty Center retail store. Her ideas and suggestions have helped us improve our long-term strategy as well as our day-to-day operations. She has a strong knowledge of what is needed to be successful in a retail business and is always willing to share this knowledge with others.

Linda & John Steele
Avon Store owners

Elizabeth transforms what many business owners see as obstacles into opportunities. She continually evaluates and refines her processes so as to create a more profitable and pleasurable business environment for all involved.

Tony Moeller
President, Integrity Investment Advisors, LLC
www.integrity-advisory.com

DEDICATION

This book is dedicated to you — the reader — someone who is trying to make a better life for themselves and their family. I wish you all the luck in your endeavors.

And by luck, I mean tons of hard work with the right opportunity.

CONTENTS

❖

INTRODUCTION

❖

"**S**he must be lucky."

Every time I hear that, I take it as a compliment. Clearly, I have made the difficult work of running a retail store look so easy that others can only attribute my success to luck. The fact is, the path to where I am now has been long and difficult – but well worth the reward.

To understand how I got where I am, let's start at the beginning. In 2003 I was laid off, along with thousands of others, from my job with a major telecommunications company. I watched people left and right of me lose their homes and cars. Some would find jobs, but at such low wages they still couldn't pay the bills.

As I was half-way through my MBA at the time, I decided to start my own business as an independent home inspector. You read that right, a home inspector. After three months of tireless planning, the training I needed to get going was put on hold indefinitely. With only two weeks of unemployment left, I had to find a way to bring in money *immediately*. I thought about getting a job, but I knew I would take a huge pay cut. With two small children, ages 4 and 7, after paying for daycare, I calculated I would work full-time to bring home maybe $500 a month. I decided to stick with my original plan of starting my own business. I only needed to make $500 a month to equal my take-home pay from working full time outside the home.

I told my husband I would sell Avon products. At least I'd have money in my hands within two weeks. He said, "Just do something."

This is when I hit my first streak of good luck – fueled by 40 hours a week of work. My district sales manager had several hundred extra brochures on hand. She let me have them to go door-to-door in my neighborhood. I worked my neighborhood and then went on to the next, and the next, and the next. Within one month, I had knocked on over 1,000 doors in my little town.

Why would I go door-to-door? I had no job. I was new in town. I had recently moved there when I married my husband George. In fact, when I started selling Avon, I only knew two people in town – my neighbors on both sides. To this day, neither has ever bought from me. I'm not knocking them, but pointing out you have to get out of your comfort zone to find your customers.

In the next six months, I achieved President's Club ($10,000 in sales), Advanced Unit Leader (the name for the second tier of team building back then). I won a cruise to Key West and Cozumel. I even landed on the front cover of Avon's then in-house magazine *Dreams*. If I heard of a new method or technique to increase sales or find team members, I tried it. That's when I first started hearing, "She must be lucky."

When Avon flew me to New York for the cover shoot of *Dreams*, I met four other new stars with Avon. One of the ladies had an Avon Sales & Training Center. I was so intrigued I looked into the idea further. When I returned home I decided to open my own. It did not go well. My husband and I lost money every month we were open. However, that little practice run gave me the confidence I needed to go all out and open a fully-approved Licensed Avon Beauty Center – in a better location of course!

The Licensed Avon Store did not perform well in the beginning. My first day open, I sold $50 worth of products. My second day open, I sold $25. In the first month, we barely sold more than the cost of our rent. Traffic was incredibly slow. I attribute much of that to my lack of knowledge about what it takes to open a retail location. Somehow I thought my MBA would carry me through. I didn't know it at the time, but I was earning my "real-life" MBA.

Then I had another streak of luck! After six months of working 90-100 hours a week, reaching out to experts for help, and obtaining a loan from the SBDC (Small Business Development Center), the store started breaking even. Yeah! I was able to hire some help. I even started to pay myself a small salary. I would have made more money working part time at a McDonalds, but at least I was getting paid!

The first few years were super tough, but things got better.

As of spring 2016, my main store has been open 11 years. My second store has been open two years. I was named Existing Business of the Year by my area SBDC in 2008. I was named an Avon Woman of Enterprise in 2010 (a national award). I make way more money than I did as an IT professional. I have a store manager on salary and a sales staff of eight. For the most part, I only need to work in the stores a couple of days a week to complete the retail work I have kept for myself.

With my extra time I'm able to run a consulting business that entails speaking engagements, helping other's grow their businesses, and even the time to write this book. More importantly, I have more time for my family, something very precious to me. My two small children have grown up and moved out (if you're doing the math, the youngest one started college a couple of years early). I now have my eight year old son and the two year old daughter we adopted at home.

I want you to achieve your goals and dreams. For me, the goal started out at $500 a month. I know earn much more than that, have a great deal of time for family, and continue my professional growth.

I've seen and been through it all – tough times, good times, and everything in-between. I have my own experiences and the experiences of others to share. Please take the knowledge I have to offer, regardless of what direct sales company you work with, and use it to achieve your goals and dreams. That is my highest wish for you.

KNOW THE END
BEFORE YOU BEGIN

❖

 If you don't know where you're going, how do you expect to get there?

— Chinese Proverb

Before we go out to buy a car, we tend to give it a great deal of thought. By the time we arrive at the car lot, we generally know the make, model, version, and even color car we want. The budget has been locked down tight. We're not going to let any slick-talking salesman upsell us a car we know we can't afford. Seriously, the decision of which car to buy can affect us for five to ten years.

The decision of starting a business can affect you just as much, if not more so. Think about it, let's say your goal is to earn $500 a month to allow you to stay home with your children. If it works out – great! You get to raise your children and be there for their early childhood milestones. If it doesn't work out, your children go to daycare while you spend your day helping someone else (your boss) achieve their goals and dreams. Do yourself and your family a favor and give more thought to how you build your business than you do when you're buying a car. The next five questions will help you define what you want out of your business so you're better prepared when it comes time to hit the ground running.

WHAT DO YOU WANT YOUR BUSINESS TO PROVIDE FOR YOU PERSONALLY?

The question seems simple enough. The answer might seem self-evident – to make money, of course. But no. There are many more reasons than that. Honestly, there are as many reasons to open a store as there are people out there.

Take the time to figure out your *why* for starting a business. Perhaps you love our product line so much that you started your business for a personal discount. Maybe this is your way to be your own boss, no longer working for *the man*. Maybe you just need $300 more a month to make ends meet (and avoid getting a second job). It could be you just need the extra money for a few years for a kid to put through college, a new car to buy. Perhaps you would like to make a living, and then some.

I had one lady on my team for nearly a decade who did not join for money. In fact, she already had quite a bit of money. However, as a stay at home mother and wife, she wanted something to call her own. Something where she could say, "I did that." She sold well over $10,000 a year, won prizes, and built a team. All of her earnings went into an account where she could watch her earnings grow.

However, if money is your reason, make sure to write down how much of it you want or need, by when, and what you plan on doing with it. That's your why – what you will gain by having that money. When you know what you want your business to provide for you, you will make better decisions on how you build that business.

HOW MUCH MONEY ARE YOU WILLING TO INVEST?

Starting a direct sales business can cost as little as $15 (with Avon) or as much as $3,000 if you buy the mega starter packs in several companies I know of. For many people, the questions isn't so much what are you willing to invest, but how much are you able to invest.

Buying the kit to get started is one thing. Spending more to try the different methods of selling is another. If you would love to work a booth at an event, make sure you have the cash on hand to pay for the event fee, tables and display materials, and product on hand. If you do not have the money to pay for all of that upfront (without being dependent on the sales from the event for all the checks to clear), then you should not try that method. Please stay within your budget. If money is super tight, try the free or low-cost methods first. Once you are earning the money you need and have extra, stash the extra away until you have enough to try the methods that require more upfront money.

When you're trying a new method of selling, write out as detailed a list of costs as possible. Then, add a buffer of 20-50%. Invariably, there will be some surprise cost you hadn't thought to include. Better to have money left over than to scrape into your family's grocery money to pull something off. I could tell you several very sad stories of business owners that got in over their heads and what it did to their families, but I'll spare you. Just know, in order to avoid panicky decisions that may not be right for you or your family, decide now on your financial spending limit.

HOW MUCH TIME AND MONEY ARE YOU WILLING TO INVEST?

It always puts a smile on my face when someone tells me they would love to have their own store. "It would be fun." While I enjoy the challenge that owning a business offers, I don't know that I would call it unending fun. Anyone who says that hasn't worked 90-100 hours a week for months on end for no pay. Yes, that's what it took to get my store up off the ground and running.

Now, obviously my situation is on the extreme end of things. There are many people who really only have one hour a day to work their business – their lunch hour at work. I've heard of many people who have built successful businesses starting with just their lunch hour.

Your time most likely lies somewhere between the two extremes. Think about your free time. Do you work a job full time? Where could you find the time to work on your business? Let's say, between working full time, your kid's karate classes, Friday night date night, and church activities on Sunday, you see you have two week nights and Saturdays to work on your business. Great.

Now, match up how much money you want to make with your free time. Perhaps you realize you could achieve your goals just by working

Shift schedule to accommodate

— 7 —

Wednesday nights and Saturday afternoons. Perhaps you have much greater needs (bills) and you realize you need to get your husband to take the kids to karate, eat lunch at your desk, and tell the church to find a new Sunday school teacher to find the time you need.

Everyone's solution will be different. Just make sure you carve out the time needed to meet your goals. Write it in on your calendar like you would a shift at work. Let everyone in your home know, on Wednesday nights from 6-8pm you need time to yourself to work on your business. Some of you need to make sure you make time for your business. Some of you need to make sure you make time for yourself and your business. You know which one you are. Plan accordingly.

HOW MUCH ARE YOU WILLING TO INVEST IN LEARNING?

I can't emphasis this enough. You may be a natural at your business. You may have a steep learning curve. Either way, be prepared to invest time in learning. Include learning in your weekly schedule. Of course, your first source for knowledge is your company's training. Right now, you're reading this book (yeah you!).

Beyond that, there are many sources of continuing education in your chosen field. Check out your local community college. Many times, they have continuing education courses for small business owners. See if you have an SBDC office close by. Many times, they teach business-related courses at a reduced rate. Join a local business roundtable. A roundtable is where a group of business owners get together and either pick a topic to discuss or just share each other's current opportunities and challenges for support from those who understand what it takes to run a business. Buy books to bolster your areas of weakness. Subscribe to a few magazines related to your industry. Develop an insatiable quest for knowledge on how to run your business.

Don't be one of the 90% of owners who go out of business for lack of knowledge. Be one of the 10% that not only stay in business but thrive because they are willing to learn more than what they already know. You're off to a great start by reading this book. Searching for more knowledge than you have is a sure sign that you are open to learning more.

ARE YOU OPEN TO ASKING FOR HELP WHEN NEEDED?

Simply put, you might think you can do it all yourself, but there are times when you might need look for outside help in order to run or maintain your business. Years ago, I came across the results of a study detailing what it takes to keep a business' doors open. I pinned the study to my corkboard. Following the advice in this study actually helped save my business. I want to share it with you. Feel free to make a copy and add it to your own corkboard.

> *A study by Dunn & Bradstreet showed that 90% of small business failures are due to a lack of skills and knowledge on the part of the owner. The study also found that 90% of small businesses that were still in business after 5 years had sought help from a Small Business Development Center (SBDC) or other business expert.*

The most obvious support system is family and friends. Are you a stay at home? You might want to enlist your partner's support to help with children in the evening, almost as if you worked separate shifts. When I started selling Avon, I did what paperwork and phone calls I could during the day. As soon as my husband came home from work, he served the dinner I had prepared and I went out on deliveries or to knock on new doors while he watched the children. Single mom? Perhaps you can share babysitting times with another single mom who has her own business. Do you have older children? They can help too. As for friends, they will come in handy when you branch out into activities such as holding parties or fundraisers.

On top of your personal network of support, you might need an array of professional supports.

Banker: If you need to go to the bank, be sure to walk inside. Get to know the staff and tellers. Knowing your neighborhood tellers on a first name basis can help if there are ever issues with your fledgling business's bank account or you need a business loan.

Bookkeeper/CPA: Have you ever seen the movie *Dodge Ball*? My favorite scene is when the banker asks to see the business owner's paper trail in order to perform an audit. The owner said, "Oh, I call those keepers," and proceeded to open a closet door. A slew of paperwork slid out onto the floor. It seems like an unlikely scenario – until you own your own business.

When I opened my sales and training center, I figured that since I had my MBA, I would do just fine with organizing my paperwork and keeping track of all the important numbers. Six months later, I had a box full of "keepers." That was the most difficult year of tax preparation I'd ever been through. My husband and I spent more than forty hours sorting little pieces of paper and trying to make sense of the piles before us.

When I opened my actual store, I hired a bookkeeper before I even opened my doors. I know myself: I know I need someone else to do the paperwork for me or it will never get done.

You may think, "But I'm just selling essential oils on a part-time basis, I don't need bookkeeping help." That may be, but once you start selling using baskets, working booths at events, or holding parties, you'll have all kinds of miscellaneous pieces of paper floating around. Receipts from Hobby Lobby for baskets, rental fees for your booth, or a Wal-Mart receipt for plastic cups for the party – they just add up. If you aren't the type to stay on top of all your expenses, enlist your partner or a friend for help. If the pieces of paper become too big for you or your informal help, consider hiring a bookkeeper to sort it all out. You never know, one of your customers may have a background in bookkeeping. While most people like to be paid in money, you might find someone willing to barter with you.

Insurance agent: I am hesitant to advise in any way in this matter – except to say you should probably visit your local insurance agent to see if you need additional insurance for your business. Many places require you to have a million dollar insurance policy if you want to have a booth at their event. The cost for a one or two day policy is usually minimal. If you intend to set up a boutique in a spare bedroom or set up a mini-mart of beauty products in your basement, you should strongly consider obtaining the appropriate insurance for operating a business in your home. When in doubt, give your insurance agent a call.

Business Coach: Remember the study mentioned a few pages back by Dunn & Bradstreet? If you want to succeed, you need a coach or consultant to help guide you in the right direction. For many of you, the person who helped you get started in your company will be the perfect help. However, sometimes the person who helped you get in is just as new as you, or they live far away, or they stop selling shortly after you get started! While there is tons of support to be found online in social media platforms, there is a great benefit to having your own coach – someone who knows you and your business especially.

If you are unable to find a business coach within your own company, there are plenty of coaches available out there, many for free. Your area SBDC will have business coaches on hand who you can ask to meet with for help. In case you were unaware, utilizing the SBDC is free to you. Just like libraries, schools, and the fire department, the SBDC is free – because you already paid your share with your tax dollars. In addition, free business coaches can be found through your area SCORE. SCORE is a non-profit organization that was previously known as the "Service Corps of Retired Executives." Now they are known as "Counselors to America's Small Business." They are comprised of retired and current executives and entrepreneurs, free for you to utilize to help grow your business.

While I have utilized counselors at the SBDC throughout the years, I also hired my own business coach for over 10 years, Sally Smith. I literally cried when she retired. She knew me, my family, and my business. A great business coach will not only help you with your business, but also with your life/business balance. As an entrepreneur, frequently you *are* your business. And, well, you happen to also be a human being with a life and family to boot. Business coaches on the low end charge $30-60/hour. They can charge up to $300-500/hour for more specialized or advanced help. Sally fell in-between the two. She was worth every penny and more.

IS THIS FOR ME?

After reading this chapter, do you still feel owning a business is right for you? I hope so! Before heading out into all the fun how-to chapters, take a few moments to go through the following list. The answers will help you chose the sales activities that are right for you and your needs.

- I want to own a business for the following reasons:

- I am prepared to invest $_____ to start my business.

- I know my financial spending limit for trying new ways to promote my business: YES – NO

- I am prepared to work _____ hours a week during the following days/times:

- I am open to learning, even if I think I already know it: YES – NO

- I am open to asking for outside help when needed: YES – NO

- Owning my own business is right for me: YES – NO

Congratulations! At this point, you've given more thought and attention to what it takes to own your own business than most people do. Please, feel free to now continue reading the book page by page, or skip ahead to the chapters that intrigue you the most. As you read, you'll see advice and tips from other experts. For more information about them or their tips, look in the appendix section at the back of the book.

Thank you for hanging with me through building a strong foundation!

A word of advice: If you are new to all of this, start out with the sales method that seems easiest to you. Why? Because you're more likely to do it. You're more likely to see success from your efforts. Let your early successes bolster your confidence to try new methods that seem difficult or even downright scary. Please know it's okay to not become an expert in all areas. I say, try them all, stick with the ones that work best for you. It's your business after all.

THE BASICS

❖

COMPANY SWAG AND SUPPORTS

❖

The first strategy for sales success listed is using company supports and swag. Not just because it's basic, but because it's the most important. You'll hear me repeat this time and again throughout the book. Start first with what your company has to offer and then move on to advanced skills and outside resources.

If you haven't already, dive right in to what your company offers; use their supports, their training, and wear their swag. Your company put many hours and dollars into creating supports for you - take advantage of that!

As mentioned in the last chapter, keep in mind your budget of time and money. Order the swag and supports you can afford and the supports you have the time to distribute.

COMPANY TRAINING

The most important company support – and usually the only free one – is your company's training. While there are great resources outside of your company (like this book), the core of your knowledge should come from your own company. They have crafted their training to best fit their product line. In taking your company's training, you'll develop an even greater passion for your company and the products. As fundraising specialist Rhonda Henderson says:

> *Passion for your product is the key. If you have passion and knowledge –*
> *you will be successful. Passion fuels your reason.*

Most of your company's training will be found in your online back office. Some companies have a few hours' worth of training. With some companies, if you took every last minute of training, you'd have a full-time job for a couple of weeks just to get through it. To start, make sure you get the basics but always go back and add on more knowledge as time goes on.

Of course, every company offers live training in various forms. You can get some training at local team meetings. Other times, you can attend regional or national events to increase your knowledge. Every company I have talked to strongly encourages representatives to attend the larger events. As event expert Lynn Huber says:

Successful people attend events! Some of the top people in our business will tell you that attending an event can take 6-12 months off of your learning curve. I always recommend that everyone attend at least 2-3 events a year.

COMPANY SUPPORTS - PRINTED MATERIALS

A common mistake people make when starting with a direct sales business is to think, "I can do it better." Many, many, many reps think they can make a better flyer or a better this or that than their company. So, instead of taking the company flyer, adding their name and number, and walking out the front door to go find new customers, they stay locked away in their house at the computer. Hours are wasted tweaking, correcting, fixing until they feel like they have it just right. I promise you, your time would have been better spent just using what the company had to offer.

Every company out there has at least a brochure or flyer to hand to customers to inform them of what products their company has to offer. Keep those on your person at all times. Don't leave home without it! Make sure you have your name, phone number, and company website on the material. They may not call you back, but may just place an order online instead.

Some ways to keep the brochure visible as you go about your day are to buy one of those bags with clear pouches on the front so your company brochure is always visible. I've known representatives to place their company brochure in their grocery store cart right where you'd normally sit a kid. Other customers see the brochure and ask if they can borrow it or if they know a representative they can contact. I have heard of people leaving brochures behind in random locations for people to find after they leave. Whatever you do, don't leave it in a bathroom stall as I saw posted one time to Facebook.

As far as making sure your brochure contains your contact information, some company supports allow you to enter your contact information online, and then print out the completed flyer. Other companies let you buy brochures in bulk and leave it to you to add your contact information. Many new representatives will write their information out on each handout manually. If you intend to build a much larger business than handwriting will allow, you may want to look into other methods. I know of many representatives who purchase a stamp. For $10-$35, you can purchase a stamp of your contact information. It can be as simple as a do-it-yourself stamp from Wal-Mart or a professionally-made stamp from Office Depot. If changing dates are important to you (due dates for orders), you can purchase plain date-change stamps or even order a date-change stamp with wording of your choice above and below the ever-changing date.

Stamps work well if your materials absorb ink well and the information remains constant. However, some company materials are super slick and the only thing a stamp does is smear. For some of you, if the information changes frequently enough, you'll want to print out labels with your computer. In that case, you can change the information as often as you need for this special or that. Over the long-run, printing labels costs more than using a stamp, but you know your business and your needs.

But, by far, the most important part of printed company materials is that they go from your hands into the hands of a potential customer. In the overall scheme of things, you should spend much more time finding ways to share the materials than you should on making them look just right.

Nearly all companies have corporate business cards available. This is one area where I diverge from the advice of just using your company supports. They are normally relatively expensive. If you have the money, please purchase your business cards from your company. If you have a tight budget, everyone pretty much goes to Vistaprint online for business card needs. You will spend much more time putting together a business card, but if you're buying in bulk, the price difference is astounding.

An important note; I have met a few very, very successful direct sales representatives that have never ordered business cards. Ever. Their main goal is to get the contact information of the prospective customer so they can call them back and follow up. That's definitely something to think about.

COMPANY SUPPORTS - SWAG

Your company is the first place to go for company swag. They will have the approved logo, best product pictures, and everything will align with what your customers see in flyers and online. There is practically no end to the types of products that you can purchase with company information on them: hats, t-shirts, jackets, coffee mugs, shaker bottles, water bottles, emery boards, business card holders, pens, and more.

Company swag is a form of walking advertisement. It's a way to tell everyone what business you're in without having to say a word. That's why it's perfect for people that are shy or representatives that are new and unsure of how to approach others. But swag is also worn by the most outgoing representatives of them all. For instance, event and basket specialist Thomas Schrom says:

> I never leave home without some kind of logo item or nametag on. You want people to notice you and logo items can help a lot. One day I was checking out at the grocery store and smiled at the cashier. We had small talk, but I never mentioned my business. When she noticed my nametag, she immediately said, "Wait?! You sell that? Do you have a card? My mom and I love that stuff!"

Lynn Huber has had similar experiences.

> *I always wear a nametag with my company logo on it everywhere I go. I can't tell you how many times people have come up to me as I was just going about my day and ask if I'm with that company and they want to join or want to order products. And those people are sometimes your best customers or team members. They were interested enough to approach you.*

> *Just the other day I was at the doctor with my mother and I had two nurses and the doctor ask about my products. All three of them will be attending our next class. It's a small thing, but wearing a nametag makes a huge difference.*

While you can wear company swag on your person or carry it around with you, another way to announce your company is with swag for your car. There are many ways to go about this. One word of caution, if you are part of an HOA, you may want to check with your neighborhood bylaws. Some do not allow cars with advertising to be parked in the driveway. In those cases, you either need to use methods that are easily removable or be committed to parking in the garage every time. That being said, there are many ways to use your car to promote your business:

- Car magnets: Many times these are only useful when your car is parked. The print is so small, you're not actually advertising as you're driving about. The price is generally $20-50.

- Car stencil on windows: Quite a few companies also sell this option to their representatives. If not, you can contact a local sign maker to create one for you. Most times, people place the stencil on the back window. In this case, many times you are advertising while driving as the person behind you has time to stare at it. Also, when parked with a bunch of other cars, people are more likely to see your back window than a magnet on the side. The prices of car stencils start at around $5 for small, generic ones to over $100 for something larger and customized.

- Car stencil + business card magnets: This is a fun hybrid of the two. I saw it on the back of a truck of a man who trimmed trees. He had stenciling that said, "Need a Tree Man?" and then about a dozen business card-sized magnets attached to the back. Of course, that only works while parked, but it is an ingenious idea.

- Car flyer/brochure holders: These neat contraptions have plastic hooks that rest of the top of your window (which you then close to really hold it in place) and then you fill the front with brochures or flyers of your choice. Much like the idea above, it's only good when you're parked. But know that it might be harder for people to see in a parking lot situation as they are located on the side of your car. These range from $10-30 or more.

- Car wraps: These are for those serious about building huge businesses. This is when a sign company helps you create a design for your car. The signage is basically like one big sticker custom made for your car. A partial wrap can be made to look like a full wrap, but can be as cheap as $1,500. A full wrap is usually $3,000 or more, depending on the size of the car.

You can also give your house a little swag with a yard sign. Those run as cheap as $10 on up to $30. I highly recommend you buy a printed sign, but blank signs can be bought from Home Depot. I warn you though, by the time you buy the wire support frame and the plastic sign, you're going to pay about the same. Professional looking signs just look better! One time, I had a sign made like the ones you see real estate agents use. It had a strong metal frame. I then attached a flyer holder and put my company brochures inside. I wasn't selling my home, but brochures were available to people passing by.

COMPANY SUPPORTS - PRODUCT SUPPORTS

Unless you are selling insurance or some other intangible service, your company has samples or ways for you to demonstrate your product line to others. Some companies sell samples to use with individual potential customers. Other times, you can buy the products ahead of the customer launch as a way to have it on hand to show to customers at the same time it's launched in the customer brochure. If nothing else, be a product of your products. Do you sell makeup or jewelry or essential oils? You should probably wear it wherever you go. Do you sell health shakes or vitamin supplements? You should probably be taking them yourself. That's just common sense.

But, because common sense isn't always so common, I have quite a few tips and tricks to share about using company samples, demos, and products.

I strongly encourage you to use company-created samples. I am aware of all kinds of ways to make homemade samples. For instance, buying a bunch of mini plastic cups with lids from Wal-Mart. Yes, you can take the time to spray cotton balls and put one in each cup and label each cup. But, I promise you, by the time you're done, you'll be sick of the scent. My time is valuable. I prefer to buy company samples and spend my time getting them out there rather than making them myself.

Special note: If you sell nutritional products, DO NOT make homemade samples. The scariest thing ever handed to me was a zip lock bag of brown powder that was supposedly protein powder. The gentleman suggested I take it home and mix it with 8 oz. of water to try it out. It's highly likely that everything was above board, but I went home and threw it away immediately. Nope.

If the packaging will allow it, put your label or contact information on your sample. Sometimes samples are passed around and never used by the one you gave it to. Should her sister or co-worker decide they couldn't live without your product, if they don't have your contact information, how can they buy it from you? That leads me to the next couple of tips.

A common method of distributing samples to current customers is throwing in a sample of something else when delivering an order. Perhaps your customer bought something online, so you throw in a sample of something else. I know because I did this for years. Then one day, I got a new customer who set me straight. She was so happy to get a new representative. Her old one used to just throw samples in the bottom of the bag. She was so frustrated by the practice. No explanation of what it was about. No guidance of where to find it in the brochure. Just some random sample packet sitting in the bottom of the bag, staring at her.

If at all possible, have the person use the sample at the time you give it to them. If it is fragrance or skin care or essential oils, ask them if they'd like to try it. Open the sample and either squeeze in on the back of their hand or have them apply it themselves. No one expects a miracle of results from a sample, but trying the product gives them an idea of the feel, fragrance, or whatnot. Even for nutritional supplements, if it's appropriate, have water bottles along with your product so the person can try it then. The best time to ask for a sale is right after someone has tried it, not a week or so later when they've either forgotten the experience or forgotten where they left the sample altogether.

If, for some reason, the customer isn't present when you give them a sample, find a way to make it meaningful. Tape the sample to the brochure on the page it appears. Leave a note explaining how to use the product. Attach a sticky note, letting them know you'll call in a couple of days to see how they liked it.

Sometimes you want to have people try something there is no sample for. Or sometimes, the packaging of the full-size product is half the appeal. That's especially true with fragrance. In that case, purchase a full-size product and use that as samples for customers. This method lends itself well to anything that can't be "double-dipped." For instance, fragrance spray, hand creams, and essential oils can be dispensed in a fairly sanitary manner. Lip sticks can be drawn on the back of hands. But many forms of makeup would be quite unsanitary to use on more than one person. This is how we avoid cold sores and pink eye. More common sense issues.

If you are from a company that sells objects such as jewelry, kitchenware, bags, home décor, or the like, then samples don't apply to you. You can only share your product line by either using it yourself or having extra pieces on hand to show to others. When buying these items, keep your budget in mind. Also, be prepared that you may not find a customer interested in that particular gadget. That being the case, you either have to return it to your company, keep it for yourself, or sell the item at cost. I learned that lesson a long time ago. Eventually, I only ordered demos of items I wanted to keep when I was done showing others. Win-win.

As Thomas Schrom says:

> *Always have samples and/or demos to show how your product can work or help them. When trying to make a sale in person, it's easier to show how your product can work or help them. When trying to make a sale in person, it's easier to lock in the sale when they visually see how it works!*

Once armed with your company's training, a cool shirt, and a bag of samples, it's time to get out in the big bad world and sell to everyone! Well, at least to someone anyway. Learning to sell to another human in a one-on-one situation is a foundational skill everyone must learn.

SELLING ONE-ON-ONE

❖

I don't know how many people have told me, "I could never start a direct sales business. I don't know the first thing about selling to people." Actually, my mom comes to mind. She just said those words to me a few months ago. But then, I've heard it out of many people's mouths. Let me tell you, selling is a learned skill. So with training and effort, you too can sell something to another human being.

I'll be honest, I'm not going to go into in-depth training on every aspect of how to sell. Your company should have covered those basics. If they didn't, dig further in their online training or find a new company. What I want to cover in this chapter is an advanced form of selling, consultative selling, sprinkled with hints and tips to help you along the way.

Consultative selling is when you first find out what someone needs and then match their needs with the right product in your company's line. Consultative selling leads to higher sales and stronger customer loyalty because they know you have their best interest in mind. Before I start in with the check lists and tips, I want to share the thoughts of Dr. Paul Jernigan, a specialist in one-on-one sales and group events:

I'm a lover of people and passionate about developing relationships built on genuine and authentic caring without any expectation of a particular outcome.

People feel your passion more than they hear the words that you say. When people know you genuinely care without a hidden agenda, walls come down and doors open.

The important thing to remember about consultative selling is that it's all about your customer and finding what's right for them. If you take the steps I'm about to share with the attitude above, then you will have long-term sales success in one-on-one selling.

In order to properly carry out consultative selling, you must have these three things in place:

1. Know your industry: basic information, tips and tricks and such.

2. Know your company's product line like the back of your hand.

3. Know your customer: ask good questions to really hear their needs.

Let's dig in a little deeper into what each section means.

KNOW YOUR INDUSTRY

When I say you should know about your industry, I'm talking about how your products are used in general, regardless of which company someone buys them from. You will get some of this kind of information from your company and some of this from outside resources like magazines and online articles. Some examples of the kinds of things you might want to learn about in order to sell your product line:

- Sell jewelry? Know which types of necklaces go with which shirt necklines.

- Sell essential oils? Know recipes people can use for ingestible forms.

- Sell makeup? Know how to apply eyeliner, brow liner, and lip liner.

- Sell kitchen gadgets? Know all the rules about cutting boards and raw meat/veggies.

- Sell skin care? Understand why skin ages and how skin care addresses that.

- Sell nutrition supplements? Understand why the body ages or why people gain weight.

This list could go on and on, but I think you get the point. Know how to use your products and how other people use your products. You need to learn about things you'll probably never use yourself. If you are a man and sell makeup, you still need to be able to tell a customer how to apply eye shadow. If you are trim and buff and part of your product line includes shakes that help people lose weight, you still need to know enough to help your customer use the product properly. As store owner, one-on-one sales, and basket-making specialist Jeanpierre Bongiovi says:

As you're selling, you're educating at the same time on how to properly use the products. It's the best way to build trust and gain customer loyalty.

KNOW YOUR COMPANY'S PRODUCT LINE

Some companies have as little as one to four products in their lineup. Some have as many as over 1,000. If you only have four products, well then you'd probably better know them inside and out. If your company carries 6 different lines of foundation makeup, at least know the different between them all. This is where you turn to your company's training and live events for help. Also, you may find many tips in social media. A Google search is bound to turn up a video that some representative has made somewhere explaining your company's products just one layer deeper than the company itself.

Another way to learn about your company's product line is to use it yourself. When I started with mine, I was determined to be able to explain the difference between all the different lipstick lines from my personal experience. In my first order, I bought one lipstick from each line. Just don't do what I did. When the order came in, I opened each one. I had bought six lipsticks that were nearly all the same color. Apparently I just liked that color!

KNOW YOUR CUSTOMER

The best way to know what your customer needs is to ask great questions. Sometimes, in the case of skincare or makeup, you can guess a bit just by looking at them. Even so, you won't really find out what they need until you ask. As Jeanpierre Bongiovi says:

Sometimes they don't even know what they want. It becomes necessary to ask a lot of good questions to narrow it down before recommending a product.

A sample of great questions to ask to help you figure out what they need include:

- What are you looking for in X? If you're talking about mascara, they might tell you lengthening or fullness. If you're talking about purses, they might need a fancy one for going to the opera or something rugged for play dates at the park.

- What products do you use now to fulfill that need? If the person only uses soap to clean their face or only buys candles from Wal-Mart, well that's a different customer than one who buys an $80 cleanser from department stores or only buys special candles imported from Europe.

- How do you use these kinds of products? Someone who wants protein powder to lose weight might have different needs than someone who wants protein powder to build muscle.

After you have asked enough questions, you are ready to suggest the right product for them. I have a few suggestions to increase your success at suggesting.

- Know what product you think is best for them – and the next best alternative. When you're offering the product right for them, if you sense doubt, you can always say you might have offered this other product in the line, but because of this and that, you know the original product is the one right for them. Sometimes people will end up buying the second option instead. Most times, it reassures them you're tailoring your answer to their needs, not just trying to sell them the "deal of the day."

- If the first product and the second product don't seem right to the customer, ask a few more questions. Your third suggestion is usually your last chance. You want to get it right. Once you make a fourth suggestion, the customer assumes you don't know what you're talking about. They will not trust you to help them find the product right for them. At that point, they start talking about looking at the brochure and getting back to you later.

- Sometimes I have customers want to buy both options – even when they are basically buying nearly the same thing and will receive no real added benefit from buying both. I have always let them know they're double buying and only need one. That might not make sense for someone looking to increase sales, but this is practiced by many top sellers.

Home party specialist Adrienne Patrick, echoes this advice when she says:

> *I just focus on my customer's needs. What do they want to fix? What are they looking for? And I'm honest. If what they want won't fix the problem they want fixed, I will guide them to the product that I think will help the most. But, it's still their choice. People appreciate my desire to help them.*

Said another way by Jeanpierre Bongiovi:

> *It's okay to lose a small sale. You may lose out that day, but what you're building is trust and a relationship. That wins in the long run. You have a customer for life.*

Once you have helped your customer find the right product to fill their needs, don't forget the add-ons. You'll not only increase your sales, but also help them use their products even better. Think of it this way, if you don't suggest the add-ons, you're not being very helpful. They could be upset later that you didn't tell them about said products. Examples include:

- Matching lip liner to go with the lipstick

- Lotion base to go with the essential oil

- Metal cover to go with the line of candles

- Earrings that go with the perfect necklace

- The spoon that works hand in hand with the frying pan

After the customer receives their products, don't forget to follow up. Anyone who's been in direct sales for nearly any amount of time knows the saying, "The Fortune is in the Follow Up." Fundraising and follow-up specialist Theresa Paul says it best:

> My favorite "F" word is FU = Follow Up.
> This is one of the most important things you can do for your business.
> Many representatives are afraid of it and feel like they are being pushy.
> But, just look at it as offering good customer service and looking out for the best interest of your customers. The follow up can be something as simple as a phone call, email, or text. Just to remind them that you are placing your next order and don't want them to miss out if they needed anything. They will appreciate your thoughtfulness.
> *Check the back of the book to purchase one of Theresa's FU reminder bracelets.

I am fully aware that some of you are feeling overwhelmed at this moment. So much to learn. So much to learn to say and ask. However will you get it all down? You become an expert yourself the same way you get to Radio City Music Hall: practice, practice, practice. In the meantime, try not to get overwhelmed with the process. Take heed in Lynn Huber's advice:

The most important thing you can remember is that it's all about the person you are talking to. If you set your intention for how you can be a blessing in their life today, you can't go wrong.

If you truly care about how you can best help them, it will come back around. So don't worry about not knowing what to say or how to say it. Just focus on the other person and you'll be perfect.

Now, selling in person is my preferred way to reach out to customers. I don't think of myself as old-fashioned, I just like that one-on-one interaction. But, the fact of the matter is, we are in a modern world and much of that world spends a great deal of time online. Every direct sales representative should have an online presence. Whether this frightens you or excites you, read on to the next chapter for the best ways to go about promoting and selling online.

SELLING ONLINE

Some of you started your direct sales business with the intention of only selling online. For some of you, the prospect of selling online is flat out intimidating. At the bare minimum, selling your wares online is a great way to supplement your in-person sales and even reach out to friends and family who may be too far away to buy from you in person.

I do want to add that I know of several direct sales companies that have product pricing in such a manner to encourage nearly every person to sign up online as a preferred customer for better pricing. If you are a member of one of these companies, you still need to know one-on-one selling (to get them to sign up in the first place). So, if you skipped the last chapter, go back and read it or you're missing out.

Either way, everyone from every company needs to know more about promoting and selling products online.

The very first thing you must do is set up your company website so people can buy from you. You might be saying, "But they already set it up for me." Ok, but not OK. They set up the same site for everyone. You need to customize your site to you. Check it out and make sure your information is correct. Add personal touches where you can. If possible, add your photo. People like to know they are buying from another human being. If you feel comfortable adding your phone number, please do so. Many times, people aren't just looking to buy, they are looking for answers. When searching for a representative at the corporate site, people tend to choose those with listed phone numbers so they know they can get help if and when they need it.

To keep it simple, there are two main goals for people selling online: to sell to friends and family and/or to sell to everyone on the planet they can attract to their site. Make sense? Some of you would be happy to give current customers another option for shopping. Others have goals to sell to as many people as possible to reach their monetary goals. Achieving those goals involve similar, but different activities.

To help this chapter be of the most use to you and what you're looking to do, I'm going to have three main sections: selling to those you know, holding online parties (where you can sell to those you know and the people they know), and selling to the world. Feel free to read the entirety of the chapter or stop when the information has reached the level you desire. Just know that the higher the goal, the more will be required of you in terms of learning new skills and the level of time and effort required.

SELLING TO THOSE YOU KNOW

Chances are, you are already on some form of social media: Facebook, Twitter, Instagram, or the like. This is where you will start – where your friends and family hang out with you already. Online selling extraordinaire Emily Seagren puts it this way:

> *Don't be your company's best kept secret! How are you going to build a big business if some of your family and friends don't even know what you sell? Decide what's important to you. Is your direct sales company a part of who you are and who you want to be? Then represent it proudly.*

Sometimes you need to make a special effort to let others know what business you're in. Other times, your product line is so unique that the sales happen organically. Event specialist, Mary Cavanaugh, found herself in a situation where she could get a break on cost of her product if she bought it in bulk. She sent the notice out about the price break and word spread on its own. In a short amount of time, she moved $2,000 of product to a grateful set of customers. Because the word spread out to people she didn't know, Mary found herself in a bit of a pickle with keeping track of all the orders. Her tip on selling to people on Facebook:

If you chat back and forth with someone in private messaging, be sure to write down their name on a contact list. Otherwise, you run the risk of that chat being lost in a pile of names. That way, you make sure to follow up.

One major mistake of people who have just started a new business is to "throw up" over everyone they know. Suddenly their timeline is FULL of posts about some aspect of their business. Don't do this for two reasons. 1. Someone could turn you in for using your personal profile as a business page. Facebook in particular will shut down your profile with no recourse. 2. Everyone will unfriend or at least unfollow you. The goal is to try and split your posts among three main kinds: family, business, and funny/inspirational. As Emily Seagren puts it:

You don't always have to be pushing product and the opportunity down people's throats but you do want to bring it up casually and frequently. Take a look at your Facebook personal profile. Is it a true representation of who you are? Mine shows a mixture of family, friends, my direct sales business, humor, emotions, and quotes…a good mixture of what my life is made of and the moments I experience.

As a general rule of thumb, I have heard it's best to stick to one business post a day on your personal timeline. That being the case, make sure you have at least two other posts to round it out.

For the medium of Pinterest, online specialist Lisa Scola recommends you pay attention to your followers when deciding what to pin. If you sell beauty products, which ones do your followers pin the most: makeup or skin care? If you sell nutritional products, are your followers more interested in body-building products or weight loss products? If you sell essential oils, are your followers all about how to use them around the house, or with pets, or to heal the sick? Pin the types of products they are interested in if you want them to re-pin. Otherwise, you're pinning to crickets.

How much time should you spend on social media? Well, that depends on you. Perhaps you need to set aside one hour every Sunday. Catch up with friends and family and then share a few posts to get the word out. If you're like me or many other people on social media, you don't need someone telling you to schedule in time, you probably need help for your online addiction! Just be sure to keep it balanced. As Lisa Scola puts it:

> *Building a business online is a double-edged sword. Don't spend eight hours a day doing it. Don't get lost in it. Just know it's going to take a while to build. You can't post three times in one day and then give up because no one "liked" them. Okay? You've got to try it again. Give it time — but not all of your time.*

A great example of how an online business might grow is how a YouTube channel grew for Lisa Scola.

> *I threw a video up there. Before you know it, I had a few people follow-ing me. I did a few more videos. Now I have over a thousand people that are subscribed to my channel; people from all over the world. You don't have to have fancy editor programs. It's all about getting comfortable just putting them up there. You can share business information with your team or product information with your customers. They get so excited about it! It's almost like you're right there with them.*

SAMPLE CLUBS

Lisa Scola has worked with many representatives who are perfecting a thing called "Sample Clubs." This is where you post on social media to ask people to join your club. There are a few basics everyone follows:

- No one is obligated to buy.

- You send them samples in the mail, or drop off if they're close by.

- The way they stay in the club is to share their thoughts after trying things out.

You increase your sales in two ways. First of all, many who join the club end up buying some of the products anyway. Also, you can share their raving reviews on your timeline, being sure to tag the person who posted it in the first place.

While you could just send people a single sample, Lisa Scola likes to send a week's worth of samples for up to three different products in her line. For people just starting a business, the recommendation is to start with the first five people who agree to be in the club to keep your costs manageable. As your business grows, so can your club.

Some representatives have even started creating Facebook groups just for members of their sample club. The customers start sharing their reviews and feed off each other's comments. They end up selling to each other. In many ways, the sample club groups start to look a little like an online party.

ONLINE PARTIES

Many of you work for companies that have a system for online parties. A few of you do not. Either way, Emily Seagren's 10-Step list to creating a party is bound to have some useful information for you:

> *Online parties can be a great sales booster and easy to implement. The most important thing to keep in mind is to make them simple, short, and fun!*

1. *Find a host/ hostess.*

2. *Discuss with them how they will be rewarded for the sales.*

3. *Make sure they know their responsibilities and part in hosting the party.*

4. *Plan the date. Hold the party over a few days and no longer than a week.*

5. *Create the event in Facebook.*

6. *Ask your host to invite relatives, friends, and Facebook acquaintances. Encourage guests to invite their friends too!*

7. *You may even want to provide an incentive for any parties booked from the event.*

8. *Post any product specials, holiday sets, and deals during the party time frame to get your guests active on the event page.*

9. *Try playing some games to involve the guests and encourage them to get social.*

10. *Close out the party and thank your host/hostess and guests for attending.*

A great idea I saw at an online party is to post every time someone makes a purchase and to do a countdown near the end. Throughout the event, I had enjoyed seeing the occasional post here and there about the products. The representative would also make a post anytime someone bought something. It made the party very social because you saw what so-and-so bought. Then, a day or two before the end of the event, the representative started the countdown. Suddenly there was a flurry of activity; post after post about of people buying something. Without these types of posts, you might have thought no one bought anything. Near the end, you certainly didn't want to be the only one who didn't buy something from your friend. In fact, the representative had to hold the party open for one or two extra days to keep up with the onslaught of orders.

Because online parties, especially on Facebook, are such a new occurrence, mistakes are bound to occur. Take, for instance, the blunder-made-good by online specialist and in-home store owner Sarah Buckely. Now, some online parties request you purchase items on the representative's website and other parties request you place an order to be delivered in person. In Sarah's case, she had a set amount of merchandise on hand to sell. Customers were instructed to be the first to "claim" an item if they wanted it. However, things didn't go as planned.

For my online launch party, I took two pictures of each item: one of the item itself as well as a close up picture of the print. My mistake was that I posted the images separately instead of merging the two photos into one. People were confused and in many instances, both pictures were "claimed." I had to decide who got the item several times over because I only had one of each on hand. I had some unhappy people. But, I made it right by offering them a future $10 credit.

For more ideas on how to host a party, see the chapter on home parties. Many of the ideas there hold true for a party whether it's in person or online. Parties are just a great way to sell more to your own contacts, as well as sell to new customers you would not have met otherwise.

GIVEAWAYS & RAFFLES

Everyone loves a raffle. Everyone loves the chance to win a prize. Lisa Scola has a great deal of fun holding giveaways on Facebook. You can hold them however you want but basically, you offer to raffle off a free item as long as you get a certain number of shares and likes. You pick the winner from those who shared the post. Lisa has a few thoughts on the practice that might help you when deciding how you might run your own raffle:

You can do it however you want to do it. Just keep trying different things. It's always interesting to see what people are interested in. I can give away an expensive item and no one shows interest. Then I can give away something that costs me less, but the post will get 450 likes and 360 shares. So yeah, it's kind of funny.

You have to think of who you're connecting with. You have your friends on Facebook. The woman who won my last contest lived in Arizona. I live in Ohio! I wasn't even Facebook friends with her. One of my friends who shared it must have been friends with her. That was super cool to me. You can have people like your posts all day long, but when they share it on their wall, that's when others will see what you have to offer.

SELLING TO THE WORLD

(that your company will ship to)

In order to sell to strangers online and build an online business of consequence, you will need to invest your time and money. Selling online is the same as any other business. The higher your goals, the more will be required of you.

When I decided to build an online presence, I paid $250 for a five week social media course to learn about various platforms and to develop a social media plan. I paid my web master over $500 to redo my website theme and change up the structure a bit. I do most of the ongoing work on my website, but she set up the structure for me and helps with Search Engine Optimization (SEO). I also spent $1,000 for three 90 minute sessions with an online branding specialist.

No, you don't need to spend this kind of money to get started selling online. I just want you to know that others do. If you don't have this kind of money to learn quickly or have others do it for you, then be prepared to spend a lot of time learning. Much of what you need to know can be found in online articles and videos, it just takes less time to learn it if you pay someone to give it to you all at once in an organized manner. What I'm going to share in this section is the basics of how it all ties together and let you fill in the details in the way that best suits your particular business.

Here's the simple explanation of the two main ways you end up selling to strangers who find you on the internet. A person looking to buy your product might start by googling your company. They click on the top link (the corporate address). On the corporate website, they ask for a representative. If you have personalized your website as much as possible, you'll stand out from the others who have not. You will be more likely to be chosen. Without you promoting your online store, this is really the only direct path on the internet for people to buy from you.

Search engines do not rank individual online representative stores. There are thousands of you. They don't even bother.

However, let's say someone googles "how to apply eyeliner" or "protein shakes with pea protein." If you wrote a blog post on the subject matter or did a how-to YouTube video, you just might show up on a Google search. Now there's more to it than that, but that is the way a stranger might find you on their own. As of 2016, the best way to catch the eye of search engines, and therefore new customers who don't know you yet, is to follow these steps:

1. Create a website with a blog

2. Post your blog posts to social media

3. Repeat #1 and #2 on a consistent basis

Why do it this way? If you keep all of your content in one place and add new content regularly, you let the search engines know that your website is a great repository of information. By sharing the blog posts on social media, you let the search engines know your content is relevant and desired by others. There is a lot that goes into those two steps, but that's the gist of how you work your way up a search engine's list. I'm not kidding. Read the list above again. That's the path to glory.

CREATE A WEBSITE WITH A BLOG

Creating a website has three basic steps. I won't go into detail here, but it's handy to know:

- Find a website address that isn't already taken. Check out your options at godaddy.com.

- Find someone to host your website. I use BlueHost.com but there are many options out there.

- Create your website. Many direct sales representatives use WordPress because it's the easiest out there to learn how to use.

Once you have a blog, you need to fill it with content. I consider there to be three main kinds of content: written articles, videos, and documents. Word of caution: if you are going to use videos and documents, you must host them on other sites so that you don't use up your data limit with your website host. I'm so sorry, I know that sentence doesn't make much sense to people new to blogging. Basically, if you share a video in a blog post, you first need to save it to YouTube. If you want to share a document or flyer with others, you first need to save it to SlideShare. Then, after you have saved the video or document, you will click on the "share" button and choose the option "embed." You then copy the link that is shown and paste it into your blog post.

What your reader will see in the completed blog post is a snapshot photo of the video or the document. When the reader clicks on the video or document, the views won't count against your data limit because they're hosted on a different website. You're just providing a shortcut to get there. This may not matter if you have five subscribers and only one watches the video. But if you make a video that goes viral and hundreds and thousands of people watch the video, if you saved the video directly to your site, your site host might shut down your website once you reach your data limit. Sorry, that sure was a lot of information there. Just know you should not post a video or document straight onto your website; rather, provide a link to it.

What should these articles, videos, and documents be about? Emily Seagren has a top five list of types of content. She recommends you rotate among them to have variety and appeal to the largest possible audience.

1. *Promotional: Coupon codes, promotional offers, free gift with purchase*

2. *Recruiting: If you are into team building, perhaps write articles answering questions people frequently ask you about getting started with your company.*

3. *Product: Create blog posts about your products. Product posts are a*

great practice tool for beginners. Be sure to include sections of interest like reviews, ingredients, etc.

4. *Team Building/Leadership: If you currently have your own team of representatives, write blog posts that might appeal to them. Information about incentives, recognition, and selling tips just might attract others to join your team. If representatives from other teams also read your helpful posts, you build your credibility with search engines.*

5. *Industry News: Other ideas include tips, customer reviews, magazine features, company awards, etc. Be creative...the more variety you post, the larger the audience you can potentially reach.*

Make sure your content is either original or information directly from your company. If you find yourself using content from others, be sure to give them credit and link to them if possible. I recently did a blog post about a representative who received a great reward at a company event. Since I wasn't at the event, I was reliant on other people's photos and videos to fill out the article. I let people know who took the picture (that I copied from their Facebook post) and who had shot the two different videos I included. When in doubt, contact the original poster before using their content. What's not okay is flat out stealing another's content and passing it off as your own. Not only is it unethical, but the search engines figure it out and punish you accordingly.

POST YOUR BLOGS TO SOCIAL MEDIA

Once you start creating all this wonderful content, you need to start sharing it to various social media platforms. There are so many out there. I hesitate to talk about them because what's "hot" changes so quickly. However, I will talk about them anyway. If nothing else, this gives me an excuse for an updated version of the book a year or two from now! PS – this book was written in 2016.

- Facebook – a place to network with family and friends and their family and friends. Generally has an older crowd.

- Twitter – a place to network with the same folks in 140 characters or less. Generally has a younger crowd.

- Pinterest – a place to share beautiful photos, articles, and videos. More women on Pinterest than men.

- Instagram – a place to share real-life pictures and short videos, heavy filtering encouraged.

- YouTube – a place to save your videos. Owned by Google. Videos here gain much more search engine weight than videos on Facebook. To make the most of your YouTube video, make sure to transcribe the video, if possible. Then search engines treat the video's transcript as a document as well. Instead of deciding your video's importance based on the title, they can also rely on the actual content.

- Periscope – a great place to host live, interactive video. You can share information on your products and business opportunity and answer questions typed in in real time. While the videos only last 24 hours on the Periscope platform, you can have them automatically saved to katch.me and share them from there.

- Linked-In – a great place to network with other professionals. Actually, of all social media platforms, Linked-In is the most important when it comes to search engines. Linked-In is the first place search engines go to determine who you are as a person. Even if you don't intend to be active on Linked-In, make sure you at least have a profile on it.

- SlideShare – Linked-In's document version of YouTube. You will be surprised how quickly your SlideShare document is viewed by people all over the world. If your company has a flyer or promotional papers, share them on SlideShare.

- And more! I know there are more, but those listed are the most important as of today.

SOCIAL MEDIA MARKETING PLAN

So now you know you need to make blog posts. You know you need to post them to social media. How do you keep track of all of that? Depending on your personality and level of commitment, there are many ways to go about this.

Perhaps you intend to only post on occasion or just once a week. Think of the 3-5 different kinds of posts you want to do. List the types down the side of a page. Repeat that list over and over until the lines are filled. If "products" is the first type on your list – make something about products be your first post and so on. Following the list and writing down what you did in your post will ensure variety. Has it been a while since you posted an article containing a video? Well, if the next topic on your list is "industry news," perhaps search for a news report about your company. Write an article on that and include the link to the video.

There is a general order to follow when creating a post and sharing it to social media.

1. Create the initial content – If the content is words only, start writing. If you intend to include a video, first create that in YouTube. If you intend to include a document, first save it in SlideShare.

2. Post the blog to your website – words, videos, links, and all.

3. You can immediately share to your personal profiles across the platforms.

4. Over the next 1-3 weeks, slowly share the blog posts to groups you maintain and groups with similar interests.

5. Depending on the timeliness of the content, the blog post could be reposted in all the same places a few months later. However, I would encourage you to wait a month or two. Then only post it once a week to the various platforms and groups. Make note of the repeat to help you keep track of what you're doing.

A note about sharing to groups: Be sure to check group rules before posting links to your blog. Sometimes you have to ask permission first. Follow social media etiquette by reading and following the rules of another person's group.

Make sure to spread the posts out at least over one day or over the week – especially if all groups are in the same platform (like Facebook). Chances are that many of your friends are also in the same groups. If you post to all ten of them within two minutes, it looks like spam. Besides, everyone is not magically on social media at that same time of day as you, nor even that day of the week. If you post generally every few hours over the next few days (better yet, weeks if you're posting to 10 groups), then you have a greater chance of reaching more people.

Does it seem overwhelming to have to do all this posting on your own? Well, there are a few handy supports to help you manage blog posting to social media. Keep in mind, when sharing a blog post, you may want to eventually share to quite a few places; your Facebook profile, a couple of Facebook groups, Twitter, Linked-In, a few Linked-In groups, and so on. It can be a headache to manage. The most helpful programs, as of this printing, are Buffer, Hootsuite, and IFTTT. Many people find these programs a God-send. Just imagine, you can spend Monday creating 4-5 blog posts, and then use these programs to slowly share the blog posts over the next week or so over many different platforms. No need to remember to share the post on Twitter at 2pm on Tuesday – the program does it for you.

However, there is one drawback to using these programs – people can see at the top of the post that you used a program to share. Studies show that some people interact less with posts that were placed by a program rather than personally by you. On the other hand, if you have issues with consistency or are just a flat-out busy person that becomes a non-issue. Getting the post out there in social media in the first place is of upmost importance. On top of that, some of these programs give you results on which posts were the most successful. Based on those findings, you might change times of day or types of content to best fit your audience.

LAST MINUTE SOCIAL MEDIA TIPS

I want to share a few random ideas on how to increase your reach on social media platforms without the use of blogs. As we are all aware, your main audience on most of these platforms is your current connections – those who you friended or linked to, or however you say it, in each particular platform. However, there are great ways to get connected with other people's connections.

One popular way is to make a post asking for help from those you know. Let them know if you can post your company information to their profile to extend your reach. I've seen this used many times and often, the representative has quite a few people respond in the positive. Some representatives like to make it a game or challenge. Perhaps they offer a free set of samples to the first 10 people who share the post. Your followers have a little fun and they get your name out for you. What's NOT okay is to post information about your business on someone's timeline nor to tag someone in your post to force it to show on their timeline. You must have their permission first.

Store owner and business to business specialist Suzy Ishmael has a great, ethical way to share her name with the contact list of entire organizations. Any time she does business with another business, she creates a post and tags them in it. For instance, when she has a promotional table set up at her local bank, she tags the bank in the post to let people know where to find her. When she does a fundraiser with an organization, she tags them as she promotes the fundraiser, when the results are in, and to thank them for partnering with her. These are legitimate relationships she has with these companies so her tagging is appropriate. By all means, if you are partnered with another business, do not let the opportunity pass you by! As Suzy Ishmael says:

Tagging businesses (that you are partnered with) in your posts really does increase your audience base – especially if they are a congruent business. If you sell beauty products, find a way to partner with a hair salon or nail salon and so on.

If you're feeling overwhelmed at this point, I have the same advice for you here as I shared at the end of the last chapter. Basically, get out there and do it. It may not be done right or ever done well at first. The important thing is to get out there and get started online. Lisa Scola says it best:

You can never know all you can do until you start using your imagination. That's why I love the online medium. It doesn't have to be the same ever. There's no end to how you can market yourself.

These first three chapters covered the basic strategies that all direct sales representatives should have for a strong business foundation: using company supports, selling one-on-one, and selling online. From there, you have many ways to build your business. The next three chapters cover different strategies to sell to those you already know – but in a way that helps you reach new customers as well.

APPROACHING FRIENDS TO EXPAND CUSTOMER BASE

❖

BASKET AND GIFT SET SELLING

❖

Whether you're great at doing crafts or the idea terrifies you, making and selling your own gift sets is a great idea to increase your sales and your customer base. In this chapter, I'll cover the three basics of gift sets; making them, pricing them, and how to promote them.

Making gift sets can be as simple as rolling up a few products in cellophane plastic wrap, on up to huge, elaborate baskets for major occasions. Basket-making expert Tracy Carden-Mason's advice might calm your nerves for making that first gift set.

Relax and have fun. Don't make it harder than what it is. Start small and work your way up. Challenge yourself and don't expect it to be perfect from the beginning. It takes time to hone your skills.

If you're wondering how making baskets could really help your business's bottom-line, here are just some of the monetary reasons to get started today:

- Increases your sale – a basket of stuff instead of one or two items.

- Customers end up trying new things – perhaps they really just wanted the main item, but the basket had complimentary products that they tried and will buy from then on.

- You get new customers altogether – from those who received the gift set, provided you made sure to include your contact information so they know where to get more.

When should you make baskets? Who are they even for?

- Pre-made selection for major holidays

- Custom sets made as requested

- Raffle basket to draw people to your booth at events

- Raffle basket to be used for an organization's fundraiser

Or as Tracy Carden-Mason says:

> *The best time to make baskets is…ALL the time! Everyone has birthdays, anniversaries, graduations, confirmations, customer appreciations, weddings, and church gatherings, and more. I keep 15-20 baskets made at all times for men, women, and children. The holidays that sell the most are Christmas, Mother's Day, Father's Day, Easter, and Valentine's Day.*

MAKING THE GIFT SET

If you are a beginner gift set-maker, you're going to start on a smaller scale than Tracy. But that gives you an idea of just how much business you can do with creating your own gift sets. The gift sets themselves come in all kinds of shapes and sizes. I'll list them here in relative order from simple to complex.

- 2-3 tiny items in a mini plastic bag with a gift note attached by curling ribbon

- 2-4 larger items placed on colorful cellophane, then wrapped in a roll, and secured on each end with curling ribbon to resemble a candy roll

- Placing several items snuggly in a wine glass, coffee mug, small metal pail, or Mason jar. Cellophane wrap used as needed.

- Baskets of all shapes and sizes. More on how to secure products in baskets later on.

Aside from the baskets themselves, materials you might need to pull the gift set together could include one or more of the following:

- Plastic gift wrap bags

- Shrink wrap plastic

- Shrink wrap heat gun

- All kinds of ribbon: curling, fabric, fabric with the metal wire to help it hold shape, and more

- Gift tags

- Business cards or labels with contact information

- Glue dots (to help hold products in place)

- Newspaper (for bottom fill and to help hold products in place)

- Cardboard (custom cut to fit basket and custom insert holes for products to hold everything in place)

- Tape, "transparent" holds the best, or can use double-stick

- Tissue paper

- Shredded crinkle paper or plastic

- Candy of the season

- Miscellaneous decorative items to go along with the event

- Outside products from other stores that fit the theme of the basket

One of mine, and Thomas Schrom's, biggest learning curves was to remember to secure the items in the basket as you create it! As he advises:

Nothing is sadder than assembling a beautiful gift basket, only to have it look a hot mess before you can even deliver. Make sure to shrink wrap or tape or somehow secure your products accordingly to prevent them from flopping and falling around once assembled.

I polled several gift making specialists and all seem to purchase craft materials from different places. Check out their list to see if one of the locations is near you. If not, there are a few online shopping options.

- Dollar Tree/Family Dollar/Dollar General

- Dollar sections of Wal-Mart and Target

- Michaels

- Hobby Lobby

- Party City (in person or online)

- Nashville Wraps (online)

- Oriental Trading Company (online)

Jeanpierre Bongiovi has great advice for when to purchase your supplies:

Shop for materials a year in advance. For instance, the best time to buy baskets and such for Valentine's Day is after the holiday is over and everything is deeply discounted.

Okay, you're set with your basket and basket-making materials. Now is the time to fill them! You can stick with only using your company's products, or you can add fun fillers such as candy for Valentine's Day and Christmas. Tracy Carden-Mason will add items such as candles or picture frames for Mother's Day baskets, along with her company's products. Whether you use extra products you have on hand or purchase new products specifically to make the baskets, just make sure they make sense together. Some companies carry one main line of products. Others have a multitude of product lines. While I have seen many baskets that carry products from many categories (makeup with fragrance with jewelry), Jeanpierre Bongiovi advises against the practice:

Don't mix categories in pre-made baskets. That's just too particular. Someone may like one product line, but not the other and you lose the sale. The only time you should cross categories in a basket is for ones that are custom-made.

I polled every one of my specialists on how much time it takes to make a gift set or basket. I expected to get roughly the same answer from everyone. I couldn't have been more wrong. I want to share each person's response. You'll not only learn how much time it takes each person, but how they go about making the baskets themselves.

Elizabeth Demas:
A basket might take 15-35 minutes, depending on how hard a time I'm having keeping the products in their place so I know it's safe to put it in the plastic bag.

Jeanpierre Bongiovi:
If I'm making one by itself, it might take 10 minutes. If I'm making a set of them, each basket might take only 3-4 minutes each. The key is to prep the space in advance and make them in assembly-line fashion.

Thomas Schrom:
Basket-making time can vary between 10-30 minutes. It depends on the size of the basket and if you're shrink wrapping or not.

Tracy Carden-Mason:
I can make a basket in as little as five minutes all the way up to an hour, depending on the size of the basket and the complexity. At times, I make simple baskets using cups and wine glasses of all sizes. It starts from there all the way up to complex baskets that have lights in them.

PRICING THE GIFT SET

Once you have the basket made, it's time to determine a price. Believe it or not, this is the place where most representatives get stuck. To me, the answer seems easy - the customer price of the products, plus the cost of the materials plus a few of bucks for your time (depending on the size/complexity of your basket). Depending on which specialist you asked, the labor upcharge might be as low as $2.50 (on a $5 gift set), but generally varied from $4-$10, depending again on the size and complexity of the project. Tracy Carden-Mason has an extra charge as a bit of insurance to protect her investment of time and money.

> *I charge an extra $3 on top of price + materials + labor. That extra $3 charge gives me wiggle room to offer a discount for buying multiple baskets. Or, should a basket have trouble selling, I can put it on sale with compromising what I put in to make the basket in the first place.*

As simple as that seems, there are other factors that can affect price and the willingness of others to purchase your creation; the main factor being the quality of your basket. As Jeanpierre Bongiovi puts it:

> *Low Thought = Low Look = Low Value*
> *Remember that this is your business and how you make the basket reflects on you. If you use high quality materials, you raise the image of yourself and your company. Done properly, your basket could look of department-store quality and you could price accordingly.*

PROMOTING AND SELLING THE GIFT SET

So you've made the gorgeous gift basket and priced it to sell! Now you just need to find a buyer. Great ways to promote your gift baskets are on social media. You can post examples yourself or have customers post the pictures of the baskets while tagging you in the post. Another great way is to have a sample basket on you while visiting customers in person. Tracy Carden-Mason takes these ideas to the next level.

I have the purchaser like my business page and/or friend me on Facebook as I post all pictures of my baskets on Facebook. I also ask the customer if I can post pictures of my baskets on their Facebook timeline so their friends can see my baskets. If one of their friends purchases baskets from me, I give them a prize.

I have listed my home on Google as "Tracy's Avon & Custom Gifts." I have customers check in when they pick up their products and baskets. Every post I make on Facebook, I tag "Tracy's Avon & Custom Gifts" so that I move up the ranks with Google.

I also take baskets with me when I do Avon deliveries to show my customers and for them to purchase. I even take baskets into the stores with me when I am purchasing supplies. I have actually sold baskets to Wal-Mart employees and customers while shopping for supplies!

You can advertise that custom baskets will be made up on request or you could have bunches on hand. Everyone agrees the holidays are the best time to have pre-made baskets. Jeanpierre Bongiovi has advice on the timing of promoting your baskets for the two major basket holidays of the year, Valentine's Day and Christmas:

The best time to start promoting your Valentine's Day baskets is the 3rd week of January. Basically you need to let the customers know you are an option. However, pretty much all of your sales will happen in those four days leading up to the big day.

As for Christmas time, you need to have all of your baskets completed before Thanksgiving. After then, you're too busy selling and your own family time to make new ones. If they don't all sell by Christmas, keep a few around because they still sell into the second week of January for those celebrating a late Christmas with family.

Of course, part of the bonus of gift sets is that the sale doesn't have to end with the initial purchase. There are a myriad of ways to turn that one sale into repeat sales with those who received the gift. The simplest way to do this is to include your business card or a label with your contact information somewhere on the basket. Jeanpierre Bongiovi takes it a step further by adding a coupon for the recipient:

> *I will include a coupon inside the basket that says something like, "If you loved the products you received from your special someone, present this coupon and get 10% off your first purchase." Another option is to offer 20% off one item. The point is to get them to come back to you for more of what they received as a gift.*

Of course, as with any part of our business, things can go wrong. Tracy Carden-Mason learned this one hot Spring day:

> *I was setting up to sell baskets for Mother's Day at a corner store. It was extremely hot. I had a customer walk up and ask if he got a discount for the melted candles I had added as extra decor in the basket. I did give him a discount. Don't forget that your products and extras can melt in hot temperatures.*

SPECIAL NOTE ON BASKETS

Let's say you're one of those that likes the idea of selling gift baskets as a theory, but you don't have one crafty bone in your body and no desire to develop it. There is still a way to use a basket to increase your sales. I call it an "overstock" basket. Get yourself a nice-sized basket with a handle for carrying. Fill it with product and take it with you every time you visit a customer. Those products can be unused returns, extras you bought as part of a stock up, or a product that was gifted to you in an incentive. You could even purchase a hand-full of top selling items that people could add on to their purchase as an impulse buy.

Make sure to label or marker the product with the full price on the back at the bottom. You could sell everything at full price, or if it's full of stuff you'd rather sell than return, you could tell the customer "30% off everything in the basket." Whatever works for you. That way, you not only get rid of excess inventory lying around but also increase your earnings that week. The same idea could be used at the launch of a new product. You could have a basket full of your company's new fragrance with one as a tester. The customer then gets to try and buy all at the same time – with no shrink wrap, ribbon, or glue dots needed on your part.

Selling gift baskets can help you increase sales by selling a bunch of stuff at a time and even help you find new customers with the recipients of the gifts. But, what if you had your own customers bring you new customers? Heck, what if they even sold for you? Read the next chapter to learn about helpers and sub-sellers.

HELPERS AND SUB-SELLERS

———————— ❖ ————————

Well, you just don't know everyone! Helpers or sub-sellers are people who sell for you in exchange for a discount, free product, or even pay. Utilizing helpers or sub-sellers can extend your sales reach. While you may not earn as much off the sales due to giving them a share of the earnings, those are sales you may not have had otherwise. Depending on your company's earnings structure, you might end up reaching higher sales quotas and therefore, higher earnings levels.

FINDING HELPERS

Helpers can be found just about anywhere you look. Common situations where you might find a helper include:

- People you meet who used to be a representative with your company, but felt overwhelmed with the paperwork and/or computer work.

- A party hostess that has a great outcome and all of her friends want to continue shopping, but she has no desire to start her own business.

- Top achievers in a group fundraiser could be great helpers. They clearly have the ability and contacts to bring in sizeable orders.

- Key contact people at businesses if you engage in business-to-business selling (see chapter X).

- Your own customer base.

Helper specialist Kathy Dilley loves to invite some of her own customers to become helpers:

Sometimes a customer will give me a big order. Clearly they love the products. I let them know I'll give them a discount on their order if they can collect more orders from their friends and family. Some take me up on the offer, some don't. Some do it just once, others become regular helpers. It's worth the effort to ask.

Mobile store owner and helper specialist Julio Hernandez is especially good at finding helpers and new team members. He makes it a point to tell every existing and new customer about the opportunity upfront:

If you don't ask, someone else will. If your customer becomes someone else's helper or team member, you not only lose out on their personal sales, but the potential extra sales they would have created.

In fact, Julio and his wife have been so successful at finding helpers, they currently have over 20 regular helpers selling $150-300 every two weeks. Not every person offered the opportunity to join the team or become a helper will jump at the chance. But some do. Some just want a one-time discount or gift for finding you a new customer, but some stick around for long-term benefits.

SETTING BOUNDARIES WITH HELPERS

The question then becomes, once you have a helper or sub-seller, what do you do with them? The two main aspects of working with them is deciding who does what tasks related to the sale and how they are compensated. All specialists agree the more work they do, the more they are compensated and vice-versa. While most specialists prefer to work with helpers, Kathy Dilley works with both helpers and sub-sellers. Here is how she describes the difference between the two:

Helper: The helper simply collects orders and money and delivers orders once they arrive. However, I do the bulk of the work. I not only do the computer work, but also bag individual orders and write up each customer slip. I do not charge them for company brochures to share with customers. At this level of participation, the helper gets a percentage off their personal order.

Sub-seller: The sub-seller does much more of the paperwork and manual labor. They collect the orders and money. Once the orders arrive, I hand them a box full of stuff and enough bags and order slips for each customer. The sub-seller is then responsible for bagging and tagging each order. They also have to pay for the brochures used to gather sales. For this level of participation, the sub-seller gets a global discount on the entire order.

What's interesting is how different specialists approach laying out the agreement between parties. I personally never had paperwork to offer helpers. All agreements were made verbally. At most, I gave them a calendar of due dates. Julio Hernandez does not use contracts or paperwork in general to avoid scaring people away.

However, Kathy Dilly, who has been working with helpers and sub-sellers for over 20 years, emphasizes you must treat it like another branch of your business. She not only has a "Helper Sheet" she updates every year, but also a quarterly calendar of due dates along with any changes they might need to know about since the last calendar was distributed. In addition, each time they place an order, she gives them a typed list detailing the items ordered and all amounts due and percentages earned. Apparently, you can be as relaxed or as organized as you want to be to be successful working with helpers. Do what works for you.

All specialists agree that helpers need to clearly know due dates: when the order is due, when the money is due, and the order pick-up day. Bell Hernandez may not require her helpers to fill out paperwork, but she keeps her own spreadsheet to keep track of tasks and dates for each helper. When you're working with over 20 helpers, that's just necessary. Here are some of the tasks she personally tracks for each helper:

A check to make sure they have the latest brochures.
A check to make sure they have samples of the newest product launch?
(if applicable)
The order due date.
The order pick up date.
The amount of money they need to bring to receive an order.
She has them initial their name at the end of the process.

HELPER COMPENSATION

Apparently, there are as many ways to compensate and incentivize a helper as there are people who work with them! Everyone has to create a compensation plan that works for them. To show you the range of what others do, I'll share each specialist's compensation plan:

Bell and Julio Hernandez:
Flat 20% earnings on each order, regardless of size.

Elizabeth Demas:
Sliding scale based on order size, generally a 20-40% discount.
Orders are expected to be at least $50 or more.

Kathy Dilly:
Sliding scale based on order size, generally a 10-40% discount.
Orders less than $50 receive a 10% discount only.

Jeanpierre Bongiovi:
20% for an order of $50-149
25% for an order of $150+

Because of the size of Bell Hernandez's group of helpers, she has found it beneficial to hold incentives each sales cycle. Top sellers can earn prizes ranging from a $30 restaurant gift card to labels with their contact information on it (so they don't have to write it out themselves). During especially successful orders, the top helper might earn a tablet. Coincidently, that incentive might also coincide with a tablet sale at a local store. Of course, many times, the same people hang out at the top while many helpers plug along with their smaller-sized orders. To keep them engaged and feeling appreciated, Bell will occasionally give them a small hand cream or other such gift. This is on top of their earnings.

I do want to add, there are times where you have what I would consider a part-time helper. This would be a customer who brings you an order from her mom or co-worker every couple of months. The total isn't enough to really qualify for a discount, but without your customer bringing you the order, you wouldn't have it otherwise. In that case, I would throw in a small, free gift now and again to show appreciation for their efforts. These are customers who aren't doing it for a reward from you, but to help out a friend who doesn't have a representative of their own.

LESSONS LEARNED

Get Your Money Upfront:

While Jeanpierre Bongiovi and I both require payment at the time of order pick up, Kathy Dilley and Bell Hernandez occasionally allow helpers to take the order, collect from customers, and pay what they owe a day or two later. Both have been stuck with the bill when the helper disappears into the wind. Because of that, both specialists only offer the post-pay opportunity to helpers they have worked with for an extended period of time.

Always Offer the Opportunity to Join your Team:

Perhaps you really only want to sell products. You have no interest in building a team of representatives. Either way, it's in your best interest to let all of your helpers know they can join your team at any time. Jeanpierre Bongiovi makes a point to strongly encourage his top helpers start their own businesses. With his company's compensation plan, once a helper is selling $400-500 each selling cycle, they will make more money by selling themselves than as his helper. The important thing is to treat others as you wish to be treated.

I have one friend who had a helper for well over a decade. She offered the helper the chance to sign up early on in their partnership. When the helper said no, she never brought it up again. Over that decade, the helper built up her own sales to over $100,000 a year. Yes, you read that right. Then, one day she basically disappeared. She had signed up on someone else's team. My friend felt betrayed and heart-broken, but the deed was done. You don't want to badger helpers into becoming a member of your team, but it doesn't hurt to revisit the opportunity from time to time.

By selling to their friends, family, and co-workers, helpers and-sub-sellers can sell to increase your reach and sales. But what if you could get in front of these folks yourself? With your product knowledge and passion for the company, you could sell that much more by hosting parties and educational seminars. Read the next chapter to find out how!

GROUP SELLING

S elling in a group setting is a great way to launch your business. You get to share your company's product line with friends and family and achieve a big first sale. From that party, you can branch out to those you don't know – parties for your family's friends and your friends' families. Selling to bunches of people at once and broadening your customer base, what more could you ask for? Well, other than, "How do I host a party?" That's what this chapter is all about.

I'm going to cover three main topics about hosting a party or class: the basics, promoting the event, holding the actual event. I will also cover what I call "specials." One section will cover party games you can play and another will cover all the party variations I'm aware of – for those who just can't swallow the idea of hosting a traditional direct sales party.

As always, please look to your company first for party/class training. If your company does have such training, know that they put a great deal of effort into crafting an event best suited to your company's product line. If that's the case, read their stuff, then come back here for supplemental information. Remember, no reinventing the wheel!

EVENT BASICS

Regardless of whether you're holding a traditional home party or a more formal educational event, most group selling events have certain things in common.

Location:

- Someone's home: yours, a team members, the host/hostesses

- An apartment complex party room

- The meeting room of the bank you belong to

- Some libraries (most no, but some yes)

- Rent a space in a local community center for larger gatherings

Duration:

- One hour. Period. If it's shorter, people will wonder why they bothered driving to get there. If it's longer, they'll start wondering when it will ever end. Some people do hold two hour parties, but only because they leave extra time for people to order at leisure. Please do not spend two hours speaking in front of the crowd.

- One exception is if you are also holding a team opportunity meeting (to encourage people to join your team). While some parties integrate that right into the one hour event, others will hold a one hour product event, followed by a one hour opportunity event. People interested only in purchasing are given a chance to leave before the second hour begins.

Timing:

- Most specialists wouldn't touch the question of what day or week or time of day is the best for hosting a party as the times tended to vary.

- Home party specialist Ginny Fiscella believes the best days are Tuesdays and Thursdays during the hours of 6-8pm. When she started 16 years ago, people preferred to go home first, then come to a party and stay late. Nowadays, she's noticed that women prefer to come straight from work, attend the party, then go home, and spend the evening with their families.

- Event specialist Debra Allen takes a unique approach. As the leader of her team, the nature of her business practically requires regular events in order to grow. Over the course of each month, she will hold a meeting on a Monday evening, a

Thursday morning, and a Saturday afternoon. That way, she hopes to bring in the most attendees.

Budget:

- Take it easy! You're doing this to make money. Don't pour all of your future profits into hosting the event. People are there to support you, learn about your product line, and/or hang out with friends.

- The important things to spend money on are things such as samples, demonstrations products, and flyers or brochures to pass out. Food and decorations should be kept to a minimum.

Samples and/or Product:

- There are so many product lines out there that it's difficult to say in one statement what you in particular should bring with you.

- I know for jewelry and bag and kitchenware parties, you want to have many different products on hand for people to look at.

- For companies that sell consumable products like skin care and makeup, you can carry enough to do an entire makeover or facial, or as few as 3-5 products – one from each product line.

- If you sell nutritional supplements, you must have enough samples on hand for everyone to try. And by samples, I mean samples. You may have bought your super powder in a big jar or bag, but each of your guests deserve a fresh, sanitary sample of their own.

Food:

- A pitcher of ice water, maybe get fancy and add tea. I will tell you some parties have much higher sales if wine is served, but that's between you and your guests.

- Keep the snacks light. Perhaps something like cheese and crackers. Ginny Fiscella advises:

One sweet. One salty. Don't make it a big meal. No one eats at these things anymore. They want to shop, have fun, and then go home to their families.

- The one exception to this is if your company sells nutritional products. Then, of course, the food and drinks will also be your samples.

A Great Presenter:

- The person presenting at the event should really know the product line and feel comfortable presenting in front of small groups. That's probably not you. The best person to present at your party would be the person who got you started or the person above them.

- If the person who enrolled you is either unwilling or unable to be the presenter at your party, I promise you that it's okay for you to hold it yourself. I had no one to help me when I held my first event. I went on to host dozens upon dozens of parties of all kinds – all while in a company that doesn't rely on a party plan for sales.

A great host/hostess:

- You're the first, best person to host a party. By starting with your circle of influence, you can then branch out into their circles of influence.

- Your close friends and family are the next place to look. Let's say you're an only child, but your best friend comes from a large family. She could host your first party. Or, let's say your sister has a gaggle of friends, she could invite all of them over for a girl's night out.

- Current customers are sometimes glad to host a party. Adrienne Patrick, a home store owner and home party specialist, says the perfect host is, "Someone who can afford some, but not all, of what she wants." If you have a customer who always seems to narrow down her purchase choices to fit her budget, offer her the opportunity to throw a party. She just might jump at the chance to earn what she wants while hanging out with her friends and family.

- If you are a team builder, offer the opportunity of a launch party to every new member. I know of several teams that were built to quite a large size on a party platform – again, in a company that doesn't focus on parties. Your new team member not only gets a first great order, but may also get their first new team members all from one evening.

As a side note, Ginny Fiscella takes a different approach to parties for team members. Coming from a company that relies on the party plan, her schedule is booked already with her own events. As a woman with a very large team, if she presented at every new team member's launch party, she'd never see her family again!

I encourage all new team members to attend one or more of my parties. They learn just by attending. I tell them to shadow me in all I do, listen to the words I use and how I move about the room talking to party attendees. I encourage them to bring a notepad and take notes. Once they feel they have it down, they are ready to host a party of their own.

PROMOTING THE EVENT

Much of an event's success happens before the day even arrives. You must let people know you're holding an event if they are to show. You usually have to let them know more than once for them to remember to attend.

Ways to reach out to attendees include everything you could imagine; phone calls, text messages, emails, and invites on social media. Websites exists that will give you a sharable link to your party invite. As people register online, you know who is coming and who is not. Some companies have their own invite programs built into their back office. The more personal the invite, the more effective it will be.

Everyone seems to have a different approach to making sure enough people show up for the event to be a success.

Ginny Fiscella:
If you want a full room, you must over-invite. Generally 25-30% of people invited will show up.

Adrienne Patrick:
The secret is getting the guest list ahead of time and following my company's training on how to invite. If the guests don't' hear from the hostess or consultant at least twice before the party, they ain't comin'!

Elizabeth Demas:
Make the initial invite 1-2 weeks before the event. Follow up with everyone two days before. On the day of the event, text a gentle reminder in the afternoon "See you in a few hours!" To widen the reach, offer a gift or discount to those who bring a guest of their own.

Dr. Paul Jernigan:
There is no secret. It's straight up activity and inviting the right way: asking for the commitment and if they are open to taking a look. It is important to invite people in a way that honors them. Be diligent about confirming attendance a few days before and the day of the event. Make sure you let them know you are excited to see them and share what you are passionate about.

Debra Allen
Really focus on your team to bring in new people. Change up the topic of your trainings. I use company trainings to develop my workshops. I never run out of ideas that way.

There will be times you do everything right, but the hour of the event arrives and your room is looking kind of empty. Take heart in this reassurance from Dr. Paul Jernigan:

> *Just some advice: if you actually do the work required to invite properly and confirm attendance for your event, then the people that actually show up will always be exactly who they are supposed to be, even if it is fewer than you were hoping for. It always seems to work itself out. Relax. Building a business is about relationships and connections, not just sheer numbers. Quality attendees of a few is worth more than being overwhelmed by too many.*

HOLDING THE EVENT

Depending on the event, you want to show up 30-60 minutes before it starts. The goal is to have everything in place at least 15 minutes before the start of the party. You need time to catch your breath and mentally move into a space where you're ready to be present for the partygoers. You want to appear calm and confident when people start arriving, but bustling about trying to get things in place.

Ginny Fiscella has great advice for those of you who are the host and presenter all wrapped in one:

> *Appoint a friend or family member to be the greeter at the door and server of food so you can focus on selling. Don't try to be a hostess if you're the one selling. That's too much juggling for one person to do.*

Make sure everything is ready and in place before the party starts. Dr. Paul Jernigan has a list of the top things people tend to forget, but should not be overlooked:

> *Just make sure your audio/visual equipment is working BEFORE everyone arrives. Do a run through just to make sure. If anything will go wrong – it will be the A/V!*

> *In case someone decides to join your team at the event, have a laptop or forms on hand.*

Make sure to have your next event already scheduled so you can let them know when the next one is if they'd like to bring friends.

Have your calendar ready if a new business partner wants to have their own launch event.

Most parties and events follow the same predictable outline:

- Thank them for attending.

- You tell people about yourself, your company, and your product line.

- You show, demonstrate, or serve 3-5 company products.

- Many times near the end, you incentivize others to either book their own party or join your team.

- You ask for questions and let them know how to purchase.

- Thank them for attending once more.

Again, I encourage you to use company supports when at all possible. Use their scripts, Powerpoints, flyers, or brochures in your presentation when at all possible. Lynn Huber has great advice about the kind of attitude to take while presenting at the event:

I concentrate on the people in attendance and how I can connect with them and help them. Our business is really all about connection. People love to buy, but they don't like to be sold. So we talk about the products, share stories, and pass them around so people can try them. We talk about the different ways they can get the products. Then we go around to each person one-on-one to see how we can best help them with whatever their individual needs are. It's all very low key, very low pressure, and more informational.

SPECIALS - PARTY GAMES

Playing games at parties can be a way add fun to the party and keep the group's attention. Not all events lend themselves to playing party games, but some do. Here are some of the most effective types of "fun" that add value to what you're trying to accomplish.

One way to engage your audience is to use play money with your company's logo on the dollar bill. People can earn play money for completing a variety of tasks. At the end of the event, the person with the most play money wins the door prize. Here are my favorite ways to use the play money:

- Every time I say my company's name, the first person to say it back earns a buck. It takes a few tries for the group to catch on, but eventually they do. In fact, you end up with 2-3 highly competitive people that remain super focused on the words coming out of your mouth. As long as I have everyone's attention, I avoid saying my company's name. If side conversations get started or attention starts to wane, I throw out the name in a sentence. Invariably, one of the guests will shout the name back to me, jarring everyone back to attention. This helps parties move along faster than they might normally.

- During the product demonstration part of the presentation, you can demonstrate the product, then offer a buck to the first person to find it in the brochure. This really gets attendees to dig into your company's brochure. You will lose some people's attention in the process, but only because, while trying to find the product you're holding up, they found something better they wanted to know more about. They are so focused at looking at what's on every page, invariably something catches their eye. It's more effective than asking them to flip through and see if they find anything they like.

- Another way to use the play money is at the end. You can offer someone $5 for booking their own party or $10 for joining your team that day.

Another party game I enjoy involves wrapping a product in 6-7 layers of wrapping or tissue paper. People get to unwrap ONE layer for every question they have. This is very helpful when you come to the part where you tell everyone about your company and the opportunity for them to join. Many times, people are shy to ask such questions. But at the chance of winning a prize, they will ask questions you might not even have thought to address.

A quick Google search online will turn up a laundry list of party game ideas you can use to increase sales and attention. After trying quite a few myself, I found those I listed above to be the most effective and easiest to execute. In fact, the games were so simple that my entire "party kit" fit inside a small box. I had the top five products I wanted to talk about, some play money, a door prize wrapped 7 times, and a handful of pens and order forms. Otherwise, I just made sure to bring current company brochures for people to look through and starter kits for those who might want to join my team. People had fun, there was tons of laughter, and the party always finished on time. But you will have to find what works for you.

SPECIALS - NON-TRADITIONAL PARTY TYPES

Not interested in holding a traditional party or even an educational event? Well, you have plenty of other options available.

Meet for Coffee Parties: These are becoming increasingly popular to meet the needs of those who neither have the time nor interest in attending a party at night or on the evenings when they would rather spend it with family. You generally follow the same format as a regular party, but in a very truncated form over the customer's lunch hour. The meetings can be one on one, or a situation where a group is invited at once. Perhaps your sister is part of a secretarial pool that meets every

Wednesday for lunch at a favorite restaurant. With their knowledge and permission, you can hold the party over their regular lunch hour.

Online Parties: You can use the tips covered in this chapter, but great ideas for online parties were already shared in the "Online Selling" chapter. Go check that out.

Book parties: Fundraiser specialist Arlene Cathey loves book parties. They work for customers who want to earn some free product or discounts, but just don't have the time to host a party. She makes up a packet with 2-3 brochures and five order forms. If the hostess needs more order forms, she's able to make photocopies. You give them a start and end date approximately two weeks apart. Arlene has done as many as 10 book parties a year. Those are added sales that she may not have had otherwise in this busy, busy world we live in.

Selling at parties and events is a fun way to meet with a group of customers all at one time. Imagine if you could sell to even larger groups. That's possible when you help an organization pull off a fundraiser. Read the next chapter to find out how you can sell to large groups and build your business by helping others.

FUNDRAISERS

❖

You may be asking why the fundraising chapter is in the "Approaching Friends to Expand Customer Base" section. The truth is, the best place to find your first fundraiser is with the people you already know. You can start with an organization you already belong to, or an organization of a friend or family. Use the confidence gained from that success to go out and approach organizations with which you don't have a connection.

All fundraising specialists agree that holding a fundraiser is a great way to sell to a large number of people in a short amount of time, all while helping the organization meet their fundraising goals. The organization receives funds, sometimes needed products, and increased community awareness. On the business end of things, you may only receive a sliver of the funds, but you could end up reaching higher sales levels, earnings sales incentives, and find new customers or team members – all while feeling good about what you accomplished for others in need.

Rhonda Henderson is a great example of all that can be accomplished by holding fundraisers:

Fundraising for 15 years. Averages 6-8 fundraisers a year.
Average fundraiser sales volume is $1,500-$4,000.
Average group earnings ~$500-1,500.
Best year - raised $60,000 with many groups and earned a trip to
Las Vegas.

First things first: I would be remiss if I didn't remind you to check with your company first for fundraising training and resources. Some companies have packets for you to pass out, special fundraising portals online, and many have products for sale that raise money for the company's charity of choice.

Depending on the type of fundraiser you are holding, the work may be easy or harder than you thought. Traditional fundraisers are not as simple as handing someone a bunch of flyers and then meeting them a week later to collect piles of orders and money. You have work to do before, during, and after the fundraiser is done. That being said, fundraisers can happen in many forms, not just a traditional, girls-selling-cookies style.

The easiest way to stick your toe in the water is to engage existing customers in a fundraiser of your own. This option lets customers know that you are a resource for fundraising. The types listed below don't require much more time or effort on top of what you are already doing. The cost to you is none or minimal. Some of the types of quick fundraisers include:

- Set a goal with your customers to sell X number of your company's fundraiser product. This is when your company sells an item and they give the money raised to the foundation of your choice. Your company might sell a bracelet to battle breast cancer, a stuffed animal to support children in foster care, or a mini bag to support causes that empower women.

- Chose a charity dear to your heart and donate a portion of your next sale to that charity. Of course, let your customers know that X% of their purchase will go to your charity's cause. I do this every year on my stores' anniversaries. The Kansas Store donates 10% of sales over a 3-day weekend to the domestic violence shelter close by. The store on the Missouri side does the same for its closest domestic violence shelter.

- Instead of donating a portion of the entire sale, you can donate a set dollar amount for every time customers purchase a particular product. I have done this a couple of times to raise money for a Down Syndrome walk and the Whisper Walk for ovarian cancer. I donated $1 for every item bought from the foot care product line. Did you catch the connection? The money was raised for walks by selling foot care. When possible, look for such congruencies.

- If your product line is something a charity could use for those it serves, you could ask customers to buy products from you and you turn around and donate those products to the charity you chose in turn. I did this one year for Christmas presents for teenagers in foster care. The fundraiser was quite touching. People would fill a bag with product and dump the whole thing in the collection basket. One woman brought in her three girls – specifically to have them buy something for a girl their age in foster care. I tear up a little just writing this.

- In fact, you could even donate your company products yourself. One year, the local domestic violence shelter asked for items needed for kids going back to school. It just so happened one of the items on the list was in my product line. For a cost to me of maybe $50, 100 teenagers got a new deodorant to start off the school year.

- Sometimes your company will have special products set aside just for you to use for fundraising. They typically give you a deep discount so there is room for you to make a little money and give a larger share to the organization. One company I know had a stuffed elephant in the lineup. A couple of the representatives that participated in that shared their stories of how they went about it.

Suzy Ishmael, store owner and temporary location specialist:
I held a fundraiser for a not-for-profit organization. The organization received both the money AND the fundraiser item sold. Afterwards, I made sure to tag the organization in a post on social media to offer my thanks for the customers who helped and to congratulate the organization on a successful fundraiser.

Alice Chisholm, door-to-door and temporary location specialist:
I sold the elephants with the intention of giving the organization the
money earned and the stuffed animal. As it turns out, they had done a
stuffed animal drive earlier in the year. The drive had been so successful
that every fire station in town had all the stuffed animals they needed for
quite some time. Instead of giving the organization money, I purchased
hygiene products from my company's line that the organization needed.
Then I turned around and sold the elephants for a second time; this time
for people to keep themselves. I then used the money from the second sale
to purchase additional items from my line. Win-win.

While doing a fundraiser on your own can be simple enough, as odd as it sounds, there is more work involved when you have a group of people selling for you. Where do you find these people willing to let you lead a fundraiser? How do you keep everything organized? What follow up should you do afterwards? Funny you should ask.

FINDING A FUNDRAISER

I can't tell you how many times I've heard a direct sales representative say, "Well, I tried doing fundraising, but it doesn't work. I mailed letters to all the area schools, but no one has called me back." Please folks, that's just not how it's done. I will give you a list of ideas on how to find groups willing to do a fundraiser, but first, read these stories of how different fundraising specialists found their first fundraiser. It's interesting to see the variety in how they got started.

Theresa Paul:
I had always been in charge of my son's yearly elementary school's
Walk-A-Thon to raise money for the school's IT needs. Well, one year,
there was construction that made it impossible. I offered the idea of a
school-wide fundraiser of selling my company's fundraising teddy bear.
The kids sold the bears and then each grade got to pick where they
donated the bears. My son's grade donated their bears to a special local

halfway house for moms who could go through rehab and still live with their kids. In the end, the school sold 500 teddy bears. Because of that, the school IT department received $4,000. The top three classes received, in descending order, a pizza party, brownies and ice cream, and donuts and apple cider. Many benefited from this one fundraiser: my business, the school's IT department, the students, and local charities.

Lisbeth House:
I actually inherited a yearly fundraiser at a local preschool after another representative stopped selling. She had done that fundraiser for years. The same lady had also been doing fundraisers with a local dance studio. Originally the studio wanted to work with another representative, but the task proved too difficult for the representative so I got that one as well.

Rhonda Henderson:
I had been planting seeds with customers for some time. Anytime someone mentioned they had a kid in sports, I'd tell them, "If the team does fundraisers, I can offer you one through my company." I told them I specialized in fundraising and to let me know when the time came. Six months later, a customer called to ask me to do a fundraiser for her son's soccer team. They made $800.

Arlene Cathey:
I attended my company's regular trainings. I followed their advice on how to get a fundraiser. I contacted the local school and set up a meeting with the president of the PTO. I was invited to the next PTO meeting and gave my presentation. I got the fundraiser.

All of the specialists shared great ideas on where to find groups to approach to offer a fundraiser:

- Anytime you see a team holding a car wash, bake sale, or coin drop.

- If you see a charity with a fundraising table at an event.

- Target specific groups in the schools, not the entire school district. Groups such as the PTA, band, each sports team, and so on.

- Daycare centers are good to approach as they frequently need money for new toys or buildouts.

- Help couples be able to afford an international adoption.

Even with this list of ideas, a consistent mantra among the specialists was to be sure to let your customers and personal contacts know that you specialize in fundraisers – and keep your ears open! Rhonda Henderson says the key to getting a fundraiser is to ask great questions and really listen to their needs:

> *When you meet someone who's part of any organization, start asking questions. Do they hold fundraisers? Are they working well for them? Do they need to raise more? I'll say things like, "Do you want to do 10 fundraisers this year or 2-3 successful ones?" Even if they don't need you right then, they always know someone else. If they do need a fundraiser, you need to find out their "why." Why is this fundraiser important to the group? What do they intend to do with the funds? It's that reason that you will remind them of throughout the process to maintain their motivation.*

Basically all of Rhonda Henderson's fundraisers are obtained from people she talks to or word of mouth. She does have a flyer she got at a training ten years ago that gives customers ideas on how much they can make depending on how many participate. Otherwise, her mode of operation is people to people.

Theresa Paul uses the same approach, but will also occasionally attach a flyer to the front of her company's brochure. The flyer says something to the effect of, "Tired of selling candy bars and t-shirts? How about you let your representative hook you up with a successful fundraiser?" She also offers a $50 bundle of products for anyone who refers a successful fundraiser her way, meaning the fundraiser actually occurs.

If you do plan to cold-call schools and organizations, plan a three-step approach. You want to call to find out the person in charge of choosing fundraisers. If possible, talk to that person, letting them know you are sending a fundraiser packet their way (and if they are even interested in looking at other kinds of fundraisers). A few days after you're pretty sure they received the packet, give them another call to follow up on their thoughts and perhaps set up a time to talk in person or attend the next group meeting. Read Theresa Paul's approach on cold-calling a new organization:

> *I drop off the packets in person, preferably to the person in charge of deciding on fundraisers. I follow up in a few days with a call. In one particular situation, I called to check in with the contact person every two weeks from June through September. Then one day she called me on her own. She thanked me for being persistent without being pushy. I got four different fundraisers from that effort.*

Understanding timing is everything. Some groups decide their fundraising plan at the last minute. Many have six month lead times, especially when school groups are involved. If you want to hold a fundraiser for the football team in the Fall, the best time to approach the coach is in the Spring. The same holds for springtime fundraisers. They are always decided upon in the Fall. The best approach in these situations is to ask to attend the group meeting where fundraisers are decided upon. Rhonda Henderson's advice, if they are unable to decide right then, is to give them two weeks to think about it. That way, they have a definite follow-up time to come to a decision.

CONDUCTING THE FUNDRAISER

Congratulations! You have (or will soon) acquire your first fundraiser! For a traditional fundraiser, you first want to make sure you have enough supplies for everyone in the group to participate. You then work with the contact person to work out the details of compensation, timing, and duration. Once all of the details are hammered out, you set up a launch event, regularly keeping in touch with the main contact person. Once it's over, you'll collect the money, deliver the products, and follow up with those involved.

The main supplies you will need to have are your company's brochure or fundraising flyer, envelopes for storing money, and sufficient order forms. Depending on how organized you are, you could include a cover page for each individual fundraiser, giving them the details of the events and important due dates.

The big question many organizations ask is: what percent earnings will we get from the money raised? Believe it or not, many fundraisers the schools hold only bring in 20%. I don't know of any direct sales company that offers more than a 50% discount to representatives, so some number in-between the two would be appropriate. In order to stick out from other opportunities, I suggest you offer somewhere between 30-40% of sales as fundraiser earnings.

Keep in mind you will have your own expenses: brochures, flyers, bags, customer invoices. If you give out prizes for top performers, that bites into your profit margin as well. Sometimes organizations are just so used to giving out prizes after fundraisers that they expect that from you. If your company doesn't provide a path to that through their fundraising department, you can let the organization decide. Would they rather have prizes or a higher percent of earnings?

Here are a couple of ways the specialists split the earnings with organizations:

Rhonda Henderson:
My profit margin is generally 50% of sales.
If their fundraiser is less than $2,000, I will give them 30% of the sales.
Once they surpass $2,000 in sales, I give them 40%.
I do have a few items where my company only gives me 25%. For those I give 20%.

Theresa Paul:

My profit margin is generally 50% of sales.
I give 40% of the sales to the organization.
I do have a few items where my company only gives me 25%. For those
I give 20%.

Remember, you want to find the right balance between losing money on the deal because you handed over too much profit and couldn't cover your own costs and wanting to keep so much for yourself that no one wants to book a fundraiser with you.

Many times, the money raised goes into one pot to benefit everyone as a whole. Rhonda Henderson finds each person is more motivated when they get the funds from what they sold themselves. This is common in situations such as the band raising money for the big senior trip. Some kids have parents able to pay their way. Some couldn't go without money from fundraisers. When each kid has their own goal, they are really focused on what they need to do to reach their goal. In this situation, there is more paperwork for you to keep track of, but you could yield better results.

Once you have the money situation worked out, you need to decide the duration of the fundraiser and important dates such as the launch event, the day the fundraiser closes, and when they should expect delivery. Each fundraising specialist goes about deciding these time frames in a different way, so I will share each of their methods of operation.

Arlene Cathey:
Each fundraiser lasts two weeks. After I deliver the products, they have
two weeks to give me the money raised, minus their portion.

Rhonda Henderson:
If I'm holding a fundraiser for adults, the event will usually last a
month. If it is for children, I keep it to 2-3 weeks. They have shorter
attention spans. If it is launched near the end of a week, I make sure
to keep it open for two full weeks and have the orders due early in the
week after two full weeks have transpired. Sometimes the length is
affected by holidays.

Theresa Paul:
If you have a regular date when your company orders are due, be sure to
allow for plenty of time when asking for orders to be turned in. There
always seems to be a delay in everyone getting their orders to the contact
person. If your order is due on a Monday, ask for orders the Monday
of the week before. If your order arrives on a Thursday, tell the
organization delivery will happen Friday of the next week. That gives
you time to put everything together and check for missing items in case
you have to ask the company to resend them. Avoid having these dates
land just before a major holiday.

Other details to work out are money collection issues such as: do they
write checks to you or to the organization? Will there be a way to accept
credit cards? Who will be the main point of contact? Once you feel you
have all the details in place, it's time to hold the launch event. Everyone
had great tips and hints on how to make sure your launch event is
successful.

Arlene Cathey:
Make sure to do the launch event in person and bring products to show
the group. They are more successful when they have seen what it is they
are selling. Also, I always bake something to bring along. It's a quick
way to people's hearts.

Rhonda Henderson:
I do the launch event on a Tuesday, Wednesday, or Thursday to make
sure the most people show up. If it's a sports team, I never launch at a
game, only during a practice. That way you have everyone's undivided
attention and the parents can stay focused on your message.

Theresa Paul:
Make sure you give very clear instructions on the deadlines of when
everything is needed. For each individual's packet, make sure they have a
sales tax chart (if the organization isn't tax-exempt) and a cover letter
of the important dates and who to contact if they have questions.

Rhonda Henderson is especially passionate about the launch event. She feels it's what really makes the event successful. While it's ultimately up to the group how the fundraiser turns out, you have a great deal of influence. As she says:

> *It's the coaching that makes the difference. My confidence level helps booster theirs. I let them know how easy the whole process is. I make sure everyone has my contact information. That way, if they have someone with a question before they buy, I can help right away. It takes the pressure off the individuals feeling like they need to know my company's product line to sell. I let them know I'm there to support them. I tell them straight out, "When you're successful, I'm successful – so we're in this together!"*

Once the fundraiser has been launched, you need to keep in regular touch with the person that is the main point of contact. If it's a longer event, perhaps give them a call weekly. For the average two week event, call them halfway through to see if there are any questions, if they need more supplies, or if there is any way you can help in general. Ask them to send out a reminder to those involved that the due date is one week away and share excitement for the possibilities. As Rhonda Henderson puts it, "Don't leave them to sink or swim."

AFTER THE FUNDRAISER

Once the fundraiser is over, you will need to bag each person's order with a thank you note attached. This is the perfect chance for you to increase the possibility of repeat sales from this event. A few tips of what to add in the note and bag include:

> *Theresa Paul:*
> *Put in a new brochure with your contact information and 10% off their next order. Also, ask them if they know of another group that could be in need of a fundraiser to get referrals from other groups they're in or from others they know.*

Rhonda Henderson:
If the fundraiser is close by, I put in a current brochure. If they are not
local to me, I include my business card with my website address so they
can order from me online.

LESSONS LEARNED

That was so easy, right? Well, when you're dealing with such large groups of people, things can sometimes go wrong. If you do this enough, you'll run into situations that teach you great lessons for how to do things differently in the future. Several of the specialists were kind enough to share bits of advice and how you can avoid repeating the same mistakes.

Give Yourself Buffer Time Before Due Dates – Theresa Paul:
Early on, I didn't give myself enough extra days to collect orders from
the school. The secretary kept telling me of delay after delay. By the time
I received the tall piles of orders, I had 24 hours left to enter the entire
fundraiser. I stayed up 24 hour straight putting the order together. This
was before I started using a contract with organizations.

Support the Organization throughout the Process – Rhonda Henderson:
I had already done two successful fundraisers with a local high school
band. I lost the fundraiser in the third year to another representative
because her son was one of the students. They never told me exactly
what happened, but apparently it was a complete mess. They received no
support or form of organization. The entire band sold only $200 that
event. They have made it clear they will never do a fundraiser with our
company again due to what happened that time.

Make Sure Everyone Has the Right Resources – Lisbeth House:
During one of the preschool fundraisers, the head of the school took
orders from an expired brochure, not the one I gave her. I was unable to
get any of the sales the customers had hoped for.

If Tax-Exempt, Require Documentation Beforehand– Theresa Paul:
One time I did a fundraiser for a cheerleading group of 15 girls. They
told me they were sales tax exempt so we didn't have them collect sales

tax from the customers. It turns out they were not. That ate 8.5% extra out of their earnings. They had sold $4,500 and were quite bummed. However, they held a second one a month later and sold $1,500. That time they collected sales tax from customers. This allowed them to make all the money they needed.

Conduct the Launch Yourself – Rhonda Henderson:
For one particular fundraiser, I didn't do the launch event myself and let the contact person conduct it instead. It was the worst fundraise I've ever had. They sold only $1,500. I believe the size that they were, the group could have sold at least two times that amount. I learned early on you have to be the one in front of them. This is how you set yourself apart from other companies that hold fundraisers.

Check Items Off as You Place Them in Bags – Lisbeth House:
I took over a fundraiser that another person had started. The paperwork was a bit of a mess. Once I was done bagging everything, I had so many items left over and no real good way to figure out who they belonged to. I had to wait for the organization to call me to tell me who was missing something. I then bagged up the last of the items and delivered them. They were so nice about it! I learned that I have to check off everything as I put it in the bag so now nothing gets left behind! I even do this with my regular orders now.

Maintain Control Over Bagging the Orders – Theresa Paul:
One time, I had an especially large fundraiser. I thought it would be a great idea to engage the participants with bagging the orders. None of these people were representatives in the company. They were not really familiar with the products. By the time we were done, there were two full boxes of products left over. Ever since then, only myself or my family is allowed to bag orders from a fundraiser. You want the finished product to look neat and professional.

Fundraisers are so valuable just by their very nature. They help you grow your business while helping others. Some big fundraisers can take years to land, but are so worth it! In this section, I've covered many methods of working with your current contacts to build and grow into new customers. Sometimes, this growth just isn't fast enough for someone desperate to grow their business (to pay the bills!). That's when you need to flat out start talking to strangers. Keep reading to find out how easy this really is.

REACHING OUT TO
STRANGERS

❖

ANYTIME YOU WALK OUT
THE FRONT DOOR

❖

Strangers are everywhere. Unless you never leave your small town of 500 people, you meet strangers nearly every time you leave your home. If you read the chapter on company swag and supports, you know the importance of always wearing company swag wherever you go. However, if that's all you did, you'd be relying on others to approach you. That's a passive form of advertising. What this chapter is about is actively connecting with others. I want to start with advice from a few specialists to set the mood. This isn't about cornering people in public spaces, it's about making connections.

Adrienne Patrick:
Make networking part of your everyday life. Do things to actively meet new people: networking groups, meet-up groups, or even volunteer. Be involved in your community.

Thomas Schrom:
A warm, welcoming smile always works for me. Start with eye contact and a nice big smile, and introduce yourself confidently. I promise you, they'll take a couple of minutes out of their day to introduce themselves back.

Think about the places you visit throughout your day: the lady at the fast food drive-through, everyone else waiting for their oil to be changed, your hairstylist. The list goes on and on. If you keep eyes open for people to talk to, they will appear. The exchange can be simple like making light chatter with your server in the restaurant and leaving behind a business card or brochure along with the tip.

While you can certainly go with the flow and allow conversations to happen when the moment seems right, sometimes you need your business to grow faster than the speed of your daily life. Many representatives make goals to talk to at least three people a day. For those focused on really fast growth, they try to reach out to ten new people a day. Susan Hamel, networking specialist, integrates activity into her life.

> *I incorporate building my business into my normal daily routine. The key is to keep brochures and samples with you at all times; in my bag and extras in the car. When I set out for the day with the purpose to give out brochures, I set a goal: "Today I will give out 25 brochures and get their contact information." This means actually talking to people and getting their contact information; not just dropping off books at a store or laundromat.*

A great way to learn how to do this (other than your company's training) is to ask to go on errands with the person that got you started. That's right. Let them know you'd like to watch them model how to talk to people to engage them in conversation. If the person who helped you doesn't have this skill, keep going up the line until you find someone who does.

Just as good, find a representative from another team who is just as lost as you. The two of you can go out together and support each other in your efforts. The great thing about teaming up with someone else is that they can give you great feedback after your attempts instead you second guessing how you might have done things differently. For wording you might use when going out, here are some suggestions from Susan Hamel.

> *This comes as natural as any conversation I would have with any stranger. I'm just friendly and talk about the place or situation we happen to be in. "Wow, can you believe how busy it is in here today? Or, "Your daughter is so cute!" Sometimes it's a compliment, "Oh, I love your earrings!" Or, "Your nails are beautiful. Where do you get them done?"*

Once I had dinner with another representative in my company. If anyone came within ten feet of our table, they heard about the opportunity to join the company. She was a riot to hang out with! For this particular representative, this approach fit her personality to a T and people loved her energy. No one seemed bothered by her attempts, but amused at her jovial and friendly personality. I'm not saying that's what you should do. You need to find a way to approach people who match you and your personality. Of course, talking to strangers doesn't end with the approach. As per Susan:

> *Gathering names is one thing, but the fortune is in the follow up. It is important to call your leads within a day or two to see if they've had a chance to look through the brochure, if they have questions, want to place an order, or would be interested in making extra money. Have a conversation with them. Don't just jump into your 30 second spiel on why they should buy from you or join your team! Listen to them, hear what they say, and find out if and why they need your products or money or a change in their life.*

If you're scared of what others might say, the best advice I've ever heard is to "get over yourself." Most people are too worried about how they are being judged to judge others. The worst that can happen to you is that they say they're not interested. They didn't say they weren't interested in you, just your company's product line. Just about the same reaction you might get when you recommend a sappy love movie to someone who hates chick flicks. It's not about you, they just don't like those kinds of movies.

Let's say that, for whatever reason, you just don't meet that many new people throughout your day. Maybe you live in a very small town or have the same route or schedule every day and just don't accidentally meet new people. To achieve your sales goals, you would need to set aside special times to search for new customers. That's where the next few chapters come in. You can find new customers in your own neighborhood, at local businesses, or by having your own booth at area events.

DOOR-TO-DOOR
AND BOOK TOSSING

— ❖ —

I sold $10,000 in the first six months with my company. Tons of people said, "You must know lots of people." Truth is, I didn't know anybody – just my two neighbors. And, to this very day, they have never bought from me. If I were to have customers, I had to go find them myself. So, going door to door is how I got my business started. I had sold educational books door-to-door one summer in college. It's what I knew how to do. In this chapter, I'll cover three different ways to go door-to-door: traditional, modified, and what's called "tossing." Any of these ways works to reach out to those in your area.

Safety Check: Please take a moment to review your situation and the relative safety of your neighborhood. When in doubt, take a buddy door-knocking with you or use the book tossing method. If you plan on only using the tossing method, please read through the door-to-door section anyway. Some advice will still apply.

City Ordinance Check: Check with your local city or HOA or whomever might have say in the matter in case it's not allowed or you need a permit to do so. Respect signs on people's doors. If they have a sign up that says "No Solicitation," well, don't knock!

Regardless of which method you choose, you will need to take time to prepare your brochures or flyers. The most important part of the preparation is to let them know you are part of their neighborhood. People like to do business with someone when they feel like they have some connection. If you all live in the same apartment complex, let them know, "Elizabeth, your friendly Wooded Hills Complex Representative." You could be as detailed as naming the street you all live on, the name of your neighborhood, or as simple as naming the town you live in. You'll know what makes the most sense in your situation.

On that note, I encourage you to stay close to where you live. Otherwise, you're in for tons of driving. If nothing else, keep to canvassing in a concentrated area. Let's say your neighborhood isn't safe – but the perfect area is a 15 minute drive away. Great, canvas that area. I did not follow that advice and went all over my town and into others. At one point, it took me over four hours to deliver new brochures to all my customers – and that's by car! I had a spreadsheet created that wiggled me through the most efficient path in my town and to the others. Even then, it just became unmanageable. I had to give customers away to make things work.

TRADITIONAL DOOR-TO-DOOR

Traditional door-to-door sales is not for the faint of heart. For some reason, it's real easy to knock on your neighbor's door to ask for a cup of sugar when you're in the middle of making cookies. It's a whole other thing knocking to ask if they'd take a look at your company's product line. But, if you're up for it, your neighborhood is safe and if your local laws allow, I believe knocking on doors gives the method a very personal touch and therefore, the most effective.

Timing can have a bearing on how effective it is to go door-to-door. You will catch more people at home in the evenings than during the day. If day is the only time you're able to go out, better to go before lunch. Stay-at-home moms get real upset when someone rings the doorbell during afternoon nap time. If you go at night, just go when it works for you. Be prepared for some people to be upset that you interrupted their dinner. I have learned that the "normal" time to eat dinner lands somewhere between 5-8pm. When you knock on that fail's door at 7:45pm and they are in the middle of dinner – they truly believe everyone else is eating dinner at that time. It is what it is.

When I first started my business, I was a stay-at-home mom with two little ones. I did paperwork, computer work, and phone work during the day. By the time my husband arrived home at 5:30, I had dinner ready on the table. As soon as I was done eating, I headed out the door and started knocking. If he was home and able to watch the children, that's when I went to work. I know some women who put their young children in a stroller or wagon and go out during the day, but my kiddos were too wiggly. It's not necessarily about what the best time is to get out there, but when you are able to. You have to make the best out of the time available to you.

Before heading out, think about your overall plan. Is your plan to mostly sell to family, friends, and co-workers? Maybe you just want to sell to the people on your block as an add-on. Perhaps you don't work outside the home, you only have one family car, and the only way you're going to have a business at all is from going door-to-door. The thing is, if you plan on canvassing a large area, you want to have a little bit of a plan to what you're doing. That way, you can be a little more systematic about where you go so all people are approached. Here are a few important things to have on hand before heading out the door:

- Brochures or flyers

- Samples

- Clipboard

- Pens or pencils (two in case someone accidentally keeps one)

- Pad of paper or computer-made form

Here are the basic steps you take at each home:

- Knock loudly three times. Count to 10. If there is no answer, ring the doorbell. As many as 20% of doorbells are broken, so you will miss out on sales if you rely on them. However, some people's homes are such that they can't hear the knock, but they can hear the doorbell. So then ring the doorbell and count to 10 again. You count to 10 to give people time to get to the door. Nothing is more awkward than being 15 steps away from a home, hearing a door open, and someone saying "hello."

- If you had to open a screen door to knock, close it as soon as you're done knocking. It feels intrusive to open your front door and see someone standing there, holding your screen door, as if they're ready to enter.

- If you see the person peer at you warily through the door window, smile and hold up company literature. That has worked for me every time. They know I'm not there to sell religion or for some unknown, nefarious reason. I'm there to sell lipstick.

- Once they open the door, say something like, "Hello, my name is Elizabeth, I'm the local X representative. I'm out today doing a customer drive. Do you currently have an X representative?" At this point, people may say, "Yes, my cousin sells it" or "No, I buy Y brand instead." However they respond, you can usually gauge their interest level. If there reaction is generally positive, move to the next step.

- Hold out a sample for them to take. People tend to take things if you reach out to hand it to them. Say, "I'm handing out samples of our new product X and a current brochure/flyer." They usually accept the offer.

- This is simple psychology. You gave them something, now they owe you something. Hold out the clipboard with the paper and ask them to write their name, house number, and phone number so you can make sure they never miss another new brochure/flyer. On rare occasions, they may hand back the brochure and sample. Most times, they write out their contact information.

- If no one is at home, set the brochure or flyer on the porch or lean it up against the door. Do not put it in their mailbox as this is against federal law.

- On the front page is where you have people write their names and information. On the page beneath that, make your own notes.

Perhaps put the name of the street at the top. If no one answers the door at #205, write that down so you know to go back again the next time you work that street. If the person says no, then write that down so you know to not knock on their door again. This method is for someone who has limited areas to work and needs to milk the area for all it's worth. This way, the next time you walk through the neighborhood to pass out the next brochure or flyer, you know which homes are friendly and which ones to avoid.

- Be sure to follow up with everyone who received a brochure within 2-3 days. While some people will call you outright with orders, others are waiting for you to call them. I always double the number of orders received by following up.

- Even if they do not order that time, continue to give them the newest brochure or flyer for at least three months before giving up on them. Some people want to see consistency in actions before they trust enough to place an order.

- Using this method, I get contact information from 1-3 people for every 10 doors I knock on. For every 100 doors knocked on, I end up with about 10 new customers.

Are you worried people will scream and shout and say mean things to you? They don't. I've knocked on thousands of doors, literally. Everyone has been polite. I have a funny story with my first effort in going door-to-door. Back when I was 18 years old, and still in high school, I signed up to sell Avon. At that time, you were given territories – neighborhoods you were responsible for canvassing on a door-to-door basis. A husband answered the very first door I knocked on. I asked if his wife might be interested in buying Avon. He said he didn't know, he'd call her over. He turned around and shouted out, "Mary Kay!" Turns out she wasn't interested in my products, but that's okay. One block down, I found my first customer. The customers are out there; you just need to knock.

MODIFIED DOOR-TO-DOOR

Perhaps you just can't bring yourself to knock on the door. Perhaps you live in a neighborhood that feels safe enough to walk around in – but not enough to really talk to people one-on-one. In that case, you can modify your approach. You would still label your materials as the local representative and walk up to each person's porch. However, when you got there, you either hang the materials on the door knob or set them on the porch next to the door. Alice Chisholm started her business that way. Here are some of her tips and stats:

> *It rains a lot in Oregon so I put my materials in a plastic bag to hang on the door knob. My husband and I would go out every other Saturday and hang 400 books. I would receive 0-5 calls from each session. Over time, I built up a list of 300 customers. To keep the effort organized, I used Google maps of the streets. I highlighted the streets as they were completed. Within 10 months, I had canvassed a 1.5 mile radius from my house with 8,000 brochures. I had to do it that way to keep my business close to home and work. My first year doing this, I sold just over $10,000. In my second year, I sold over $42,000.*

I have used this method myself. There have been times when I had a bunch of brochures to get out, but was short on time. If you skip knocking on the door, you can get a bunch more brochures out there. You just have less people call than if you knock on the door and they see your face. But, this method definitely has a place in growing your business.

TOSSING

This method is nearly like the last, but more like "drive by" canvassing. After preparing the materials, you either place them in plastic bags or roll them up and secure them with a rubber band. One person drives the car while the other person tosses the brochure or flyer onto the driveway. Some people have attempted to drive and toss all by themselves. That is just not recommended. You might as well text and drive. While I prefer the personal touch, many, many representatives swear by this method of building their businesses. One such representative, Rhonda Dingman, has her own tips and stats to share:

> *I toss 100-300 books every two weeks. I spend about 8-10 hours on preparation including stamping, flyers, and bagging brochures. The tossing itself takes 2-3 hours. I just don't go home until they are all gone. I average 3-5 new customers per toss: sometimes less, sometimes more. I also include businesses in my efforts. Many times, those calls include multiple orders. I have obtained about half of my 200 customers from this method.*

For months, selling door-to-door was the only method I used to build my business. But, over time, I discovered the same thing Rhonda Dingman did – that stopping at one business could produce multiple customers. That's when I turned my focus to going business-to-business. Read the next chapter to find out more!

BUSINESS-TO-BUSINESS

❖

A re you willing to talk to strangers, but not comfortable knocking on people's doors? Would you like faster results than hoping you happen to run into enough people in your day-to-day errands? Well, try selling business to business. Instead of approaching people one at a time, you're approaching groups of people – those working at each business.

Before you read much further, I want to talk to those who skipped the door-to-door chapter. Even if you never intend to do actual door-to-door sales, this chapter will make much more sense if you read that chapter first. Many basics are covered there that are not repeated in this chapter. However, I will repeat the advice to check with local ordinances about approaching businesses, just in case you need a permit or it's just not allowed. Also, practice good etiquette. If they have a sign that says no soliciting...don't.

PLANNING

When setting out to approach a bunch of businesses, you need pretty much the same tools as going door-to-door. Printed materials such as brochures, flyers, business cards, a notepad, and a few pens/pencils. You will look more professional if you have business cards and a clipboard for your notepad. They are nice to have, but not necessary.

Same as door-to-door, you will want to plan your route. Now, if you live in a small town, well, that's just keeping track of every business on the downtown strip. If you're from a suburban or urban area, it will be helpful to make note of all the places you've been – and the time of day you stopped by. You might even want to write down the name of the person you talked to and any information they shared about the business when you stopped by. Sometimes, there is very little to write down. Other times, employees share the best times of day to stop by, the name of the manager who would love to partner with you, and so on. Be prepared for either situation.

There are two kinds of customers you are reaching when you go business to business. The most likely customers are the employees who work there. Actually, those are the only people you should ever approach. Unless a customer of the business tackles you to the ground and demands you give them a brochure, don't talk to the customers. That is very bad etiquette and will not endear you to the place of business. The way to gain customers through their customers is when you are allowed to leave brochures on their waiting tables.

Understanding you won't be talking to customers, the best time to head out is when businesses are slow so that employees are available to talk to you. If they are busy, they will not have time to talk to you at all. This time varies for many businesses. However, generally businesses are slow first thing in the morning, mid-afternoon, and near the end of the day (whenever it is they close). Weekdays tend to be slower than weekends. Slower is better since your goal is to talk to employees.

THE APPROACH

When entering the place of business, look for an employee who isn't already helping someone. If they are busy, wait patiently until they are available. A simple, direct approach is to say something like, "Is your business already being served by an X representative?" The answer is almost always no. Occasionally, you'll find out that someone who works there, or the cousin of someone who works there, already sells your line. But, for the most part, you will be the first person ever to ask such a question.

Depending on your product line and the place of business, there are many different ways you can partner with a local business. For myself, I would approach every business. For those that have waiting rooms, I ask if I can leave the brochures there and then give one or two to the receptionist. I called it my "Brochure Exchange Program." My company changed brochures every two weeks. I made a commitment to drop off new brochures every two weeks to give their customers or patients materials to read. I also committed to making sure any of my old brochures were removed so the materials were always fresh. Susan Hamel has great ways to approach businesses as well:

> *There are a few different approaches I take when talking to the workers at the stores. I look for a kiosk or store where there are no customers, or at least none at the counter. I'll walk in and say something like, "Hi! We're from X and we're giving out lipstick today!" or "Well, since it's not too busy right now, I thought I'd come in and give you an X brochure to look at. And here – I have some samples too!" They are always excited to get something free. It's a great way to start the conversation.*

Consistency is key whether you're leaving brochures in a waiting room or dropping them off to the employees. Don't be surprised if you have few to no orders to start. People want to know you're trustworthy. Remember, you were a stranger who walked in off the street while they were at work.

One of my favorite places to leave brochures was a dentist office in town. The first time I dropped off brochures, no one ordered. The second time, one nurse ordered. Once she had received her order and everything was fine, I consistently had 3-5 orders every two weeks. The office only had six ladies. The dentist office was one stop, but with many orders.

There are times where you walk in and feel a cold stare from the only employee there. If a business does not have a waiting room and you feel unsure how you might be able to work with them, ask if they could leave your brochure/flyer in the employee break room. The person at the front desk might not be interested in your products, but the staff in the afternoon shift just might.

For restaurants, I make sure to work with the servers. I try to get the name of one who might be willing to be the "helper" for the group. See the chapter on Helpers and Sub-Sellers for more information on how that works. Places with waitresses and waiters are the best as they always have tip money to pay for their order! Suzy Ishmael has a real innovative twist on how to work with restaurants in her area:

> *I partner with local diners to advertise on their disposable placemat liners. Every six months, I pay $250 to advertise on 5,000 placemat liners alongside other local businesses. We share the costs which makes it very reasonable, considering the publicity and amount of business it generates. I'm able to track its success from the coupons I put on there.*

Actually, upon interviewing my business to business specialists, I found many ways I hadn't even thought of. Read on for more variety on how to partner with businesses in your area:

> *Thomas Schrom:*
> *I have set up in locations such as coffee shops, clothing stores, corner stores, fast food chains, ice cream shops. I've set up in fire stations and even local clubs like the Moose Lodge and the Eagles Club. Some locations I just visit here and there. Other locations see me on the same days/times every week. I post where I'm at on social media so customers and friends know where to find me. How do I end up able to set up a display in a business? I always wear a big smile and dress appropriately. People feel more comfortable working with you and approaching you when you look and feel confident. I always make sure to have brochures on hand, as well as testers for a few of the more popular items.*

> *Suzy Ishmael:*
> *I partner with the local banks. Every now and then, I set up a "Customer Appreciation Table." I have printed materials and testers on hand, but also sample sets to give to people coming into the bank. I pick up customers and sometimes even new team members. My partnership with the bank is if I have a new team member join, I strongly encourage them to open a new bank account for their new business. It's a triple win. I get a new team member, they get a head start on managing their*

business funds properly, and I assist the bank in making their numbers for new accounts. Whatever business you partner with, make sure you show them how they can gain by working with you.

Alice Chisholm:
I love it when a local business allows me to leave Avon books on their counter. I always take a nice container and have the books sit upright. I often use a recipe box with the lid removed. Just add a tag that says "free" and your books will disappear. I like to buy the boxes (or baskets) at Goodwill or garage sales, and I never pay more than $2. Sometimes the boxes disappear so make sure you don't invest too much money in your holders. I prefer to use containers for my books so the books stand upright and are easy to see.

Thomas Schrom:
My cautionary tale? One time while visiting a business I already had a relationship with, I invited along a team member who brought her unruly 3 year old. Hey, the kid was 3. I understood. But at one point, the kid started screaming and making a scene. He threw his drink across the room. It spun around along its path, spilling liquids all along the way. It was like a horror scene in a movie. I apologized and gave the staff present an offer of 20% off their next order. They won't let me set up displays anymore, but I can still go in there and sell baskets and leave brochures for employees.

However you decide to approach businesses in your area, remember to be respectful of their space and employees. I will say, of the three options in this section, I personally love business to business the most – if only because you get to approach groups of people at a time. But, wouldn't it be neat if you had groups of people approaching you? Read on to the next section on all the ways to go about that!

RETAIL SALES

❖

TEMPORARY STORES: EVENTS

❖

Imagine: people coming to you to buy your products. What a great idea! I know in many people's minds this appears to be the ideal path to higher sales. Just know, it's nothing like the movie. You know, the one that promises, "If you build it, they will come." It just doesn't work that way. A great deal more time, effort, and money is required for retail sales than with any discussed so far. For one, you are paying for product up front – before anyone has even handed you a dime. Even so, the rewards can be much greater. You gain the benefits of impulse sales, new regular customers, and even possibly new team members.

At the risk of sounding like a broken record, I want to remind you to check with local ordinances to make sure you can set up temporary stores. Some places allow you to do whatever you want. Many have regulations that allow you to have, say, up to four retail events a year without having to apply for a city retail license. I know that sounds weird, but even my city passed that ordinance to stop people from holding garage sales every Saturday (effectively turning their driveway into a once-a-week store). I want everyone knowledgeable enough to operate within the law.

A new bit of advice for me to give: look into acquiring insurance for your business. If you're doing business on your personal property (garage sale, etc.), then you might want to add business insurance to your home policy. Many locations require you to have an Event Liability Insurance policy of at least $1,000,000 in order to have a booth at their event to protect against personal or property damage. Don't let that number scare you, it usually only costs $50-70 a day, depending on the situation. If you have business insurance on your home, you may check to see, but it might also cover business that you conduct off-site, especially if it's of a temporary nature.

One last bit of advice, then I promise I will dive into temporary retail locations. As I cover all the different types, I want you to keep in mind the resources each will require. By resources I mean your money, time, and effort. What do I mean? First, there is cost. You will have the cost of products to have on hand and the cost of all the materials you need to host the event (tables, samples, flyers, and more). Whatever you think it might cost to pull off an event, multiply that by two at least. All kinds of new expenses tend to pop up – like needing plastic tubs to hold the products and supplies!

Make sure you have the time and stamina to pull off these events. The event may only last two hours, but may require loads more time for prep and tear down time. Not to mention, the effort of lugging loads of products and materials from your car to the event and back. As you read through each type, ask yourself, "Is this method the right one for me and my budget?"

Thank you for bearing with me through all the warnings and reminders! I know you're excited to just learn how to do this! I will first cover having a table or booth to sell from: places to have one, how to prepare, and how to work the event. I will then talk about different ways to run a mobile retail location out of your car. Feel free to read on through or jump around to the sections you need to brush up on.

TABLES AND BOOTHS; WHERE TO FIND THEM

The easiest and fastest way to have a table of products for sale is to set one up on your own property. I know of quite a few women who incorporate their company's product line into their twice-a-year garage sale. Jenny Kernan-Catalano sets one up every year to coincide with a local celebration.

> *I set up a booth in my front yard for the local Peach Days Celebration.*
> *I'm on a main street where attendees park and walk to the event. So I*
> *get a lot of foot traffic and don't have to pay the horrendous event fees.*

Another way to have a table is to make your own event at someone else's location. This is where you contact local businesses to ask if you can sell out of their location. Remember the last chapter, selling business to business? It's the same concept, but rather than asking to just leave brochures behind or set up a small display, you're asking to actually sell out of their location. Thomas Schrom actually does that from a few of his locations. With his wit and charm, he won some of them over to allow more than just a display, but to sell products as well. Of course, expect to form bonds with those businesses as well. After a few years of selling at the Moose Lodge, he became a member!

Some of you may have a friend or family member with a mom and pop shop that would let you set up a table from time to time. I know some businesses will allow you to set up a table if you sell complementary products; for instance, if they are a clothing store and you sell beauty products. Another scenario might be a chiropractor's office and you sell nutritional products. Alice Chisholm actually approached a location she already did business with.

> *The owner had a large floor space, but only used a small part of it for her service. I asked if I could set up a table of products to sell for Valentine's Day. To my surprise, she said yes! She even let my sister set up a second table of her homemade crafts. I offered to pay, but she was just happy to have my company and hoped I would help draw people in to increase her own customer base. I made up flyers for the event and had ten neighboring stores allow me to place them in their window.*

Nursing homes and assisted living centers are actually a really great place to approach to set up your own retail events. For those of us who have had held our own events at such locations, there is a middle ground you're looking for; those who are unable to leave of their own accord to go shopping, yet have money to spend. Here's what I mean by that. If you set up at a location where everyone is still quite independent, then if they need something, they usually just drive to the store to get it themselves. Also, some homes carry a large number of residents that have run out of personal savings and do not have money to spend. At that point, it becomes a moral issue of taking money from someone who can't afford it. Alice Chisholm has actually built a thriving business around this model. She has quite a few tips to share that are particular to working with this population.

- *Work with the Activities Coordinator to get a regular spot on the calendar at least once a month.*

- *Make sure you're the only table set up for that day.*

- *Be consistent and show up on time to build a loyal customer base.*

- *Sell from 11-2 to catch them during lunch. Everyone comes down for lunch.*

- *Set up near the cafeteria so they pass you on their way in or out.*

- *Mark prices in large numbers that are easy to read.*

- *Use bags with handles so they can hang from walkers and such.*

- *If your product requires batteries, it's a kindness to include them with purchase since they don't always have access to stores.*

- *Keep gift bags and tissue paper on hand to help someone turn a purchase into a gift. Many times, that's what the purchase is for. Without you providing this service, they have the awkward task of handing over unwrapped gifts to loved ones.*

- *Remember you can always sell to the support staff as well.*

- *To make things more fun, you can occasionally add an event to your presence, such as holding bingo with your products as the prize.*

- *Understand that no one will buy from you at first. However, once they know you're a stable presence, they become very loyal.*

Setting up your own table is all well and good, but many people prefer to have a booth at an event amongst many other tables. Why? The event draws a lot more people from a wider range than your local neighborhood. These events can be found year-round in all kinds of venues: churches, schools, fairs, festivals, and more. Google your area, post inquiries on social media, and ask around. If you look hard enough, you'll find more events than you could ever attend. Some of these places will let you attend for free – but that's pretty rare. Smaller events, such as in churches and schools, might charge small fees around the $25-$75 range. Many community events have fees that range from $300-$500 a day or more. The costs can go up from there. It just depends on the venue and how many people they expect to be there. To give you an idea on what you might expect from different venues, event specialist Susan Zabel draws the comparison.

> *For a regular one-day event, I might take 30 minutes to set up and sell $50-500 in product. I do events like that all the time. However, once a year, I attend a 9-day event that overshadows them all. I take the entire year to plan and prepare for the event, buying products when they are on great sales and so forth. It takes nearly a week to set up, nine days to run it, and an entire day to pack it all back up. My sales from that event range from $12,000-15,000.*

Flea markets are a way to have a temporary location. Some are also permanent locations. It really depends on how they are operated in your area. Some are held outdoors; some are all indoors. Some only operate half days on Saturdays; some are open seven days a week. Some charge by the day; some require you to sign 6-12 month agreements. Depending on your area and your interests, either follow the advice in this chapter or read up on the chapter about opening a store. I do want to give a heads up warning; you may experience deep price gouging and heavy price negotiation from customers attending flea markets. Your margin may be very slim.

TABLES AND BOOTHS: PREPARATION

There are a great deal of materials and resources to have prepared beforehand when working an event. This first time you do one, you might get overwhelmed and you wouldn't be human if you didn't forget something at least mildly important. However, once you work several events, you get the hang of it and things tend to run much smoother.

In fact, those who work events regularly tend to set up something like "event in a box." As long as you set them right after an event, the next event is as simple as grabbing your boxes and heading out.

Of course, to sell stuff, you must have products on hand. It's good to have a mix of price ranges if possible: inexpensive items for impulse shopping, many items in the mid-range, and possibly some higher priced items for price comparison. Sell items in sets to move product faster. See the chapter on basket making for more ideas there. If you sell consumable products (makeup, fragrance, lotions, oils, nutritional products), many times, people expect to be able to try a sample or see a demo. Here are some main materials to keep in mind along with tips from the experts.

- *Grab Bags – I take a mix of products I'm otherwise having a hard time selling, put them in a brown bag and wrap them up with tape. I price them so that I at least get my money back, essentially at the cost of what I paid. I make tons of them, but at my big event, they are all usually gone by the end of my first day. (Susan Zabel)*

- *To keep track of inventory, I use the Pages App and my iPad Air quite a bit. (Thomas Schrom)*

- *I use the "eyeball" method to track my inventory. If it looks like I'm getting low in this category or that, I order more. (Alice Chisholm)*

- *Keep track of what you paid for the products (plus tax) so you make sure you never sell it for less than your cost. (Susan Zabel)*

- *Don't over-buy for the event. It's better to run out and have to take orders than be stuck with tons of inventory. (Susan Zabel)*

- *If I sell out of the products I have on-hand, I use my tablet to place the orders online so they're shipped directly to the customer. (Mary Cavanaugh)*

- *Half of my sales come from product on hand and about half from orders that I deliver later. (Alice Chisholm)*

Many, many materials are needed to help pull off the event. Sometimes, the event will provide the table and other materials. Other times, it's all up to you. If you are outdoors, you might need a tent to protect you from the sun and rain. You will need a place to set your products: tables and table cloths. Make sure to have enough printed materials on hand (brochures, flyers, business cards). If trying to build a customer base or build a team, you will need materials to collect contact information such as a notepad, name sheet, raffle tickets, and many, many pens. Of course, don't forget the personal comforts: a chair, drinks, snacks, and a cell phone charger. If you have any reason to need electricity, bring an extension cord (or two). This is by no means an extensive list, but a place to start. Every event will have different needs.

- *If you're working a multiple-day event, make sure you bring extra cloths to cover your table at the end of each day. If you have particularly expensive items, you may want to either hide them under the table or take them home with you each night. (Mary Cavanaugh)*

- *If you are outside, be prepared for wind. What seems like nothing on a regular day is like a hurricane when you're holding an event. Helpers to keep in mind are table cloth pins, sand bags for signage, rocks or heavy items to place on top of flyers or brochures, little baskets or buckets to hold raffle tickets and pens. (Elizabeth Demas)*

- *Always make sure to weigh down your tent. One clear sunny day, all it took was one swift gust of wind. I was chasing a 10x10 canopy through a 4-way traffic stop. In the midst of traffic, I had to flip it over and carry it back to my spot. This was a vendor event in a coffee shop parking lot so I was all alone in my battle with Mother Nature. (Thomas Schrom)*

- *If you are using banners, make sure to have the printer add grommets to the banner. That gives you more options for how to hang the banner, depending on your venue. Be prepared for wind! (Mary Cavanaugh)*

You must have a way to collect and manage the money that comes in. Yes, you could say cash-only, but then you'd be missing out on a fair amount of sales. The specialists all had their own methods and tips for managing the money.

- *For my large event, I bring in a cash register. Otherwise, I use a cash box. Sometimes I wear an apron with pockets and work the cash out of there. Honestly, I prefer to use the Square. One swipe and you're done. It's even faster than cash. (Susan Zabel)*

- *If I'm doing a larger event like a county fair, I always use a lockbox for cash. If it's more of a smaller local event, I'll use y zip up cash and carry bag, making sure to keep it safe in my front pocket. For credit cards, I use the Square reader. However, if they are charging less than $25, I let them know there is a $2.95 processing fee. (Thomas Schrom)*

- *I prefer cash, but otherwise I will use PayPal to collect the money. (Mary Cavanaugh)*

- *I round all prices to the nearest quarter or dollar to help with cash transactions. For instance, if an item is normally $16.31 ($15 + tax), then I price it at $16.50. (Susan Zabel)*

Everyone uses some sort of signage to draw attention to their table. The signage can be as simple as flyers on the table. You could have banners hanging behind you or built into a stand. Your company's name could be printed on the table cloths or even the pop-up tent. Aside from signage, my favorite way to draw people to my booth or table is with a raffle. Even if people aren't familiar with your product line, they love a chance to win. Sure, you have people wary of handing out their contact information, but the rest know that's the price to pay for a chance to win.

My advice on raffles is to have signage that makes it clear it's free to enter (unless you want to sell the raffle tickets). Let people know when the winner will be drawn (and if they have to be present to win). I love to make a huge gift basket full of products to really draw people's eyes to the table. For more information on making a gift basket, read that chapter.

To make the most of your raffle, consider making your own raffle tickets. I used to have a long raffle ticket that required a lot of information from the person. I now use a small one that gets the basics (name and phone number) and a check off box that asks if they're interested in the selling opportunity. Ask for information that would be useful to your goals. If I make some kind of connection with the entrant, I make a note on the back of the raffle card before putting it in the box. Perhaps they mentioned they needed help with this or that, but the booth was too busy or their friend was walking off and they didn't have time to stay and talk. It gives me a chance to properly follow up later. For my peace of mind, I have a stranger pick a winner (and alternate just in case). I like the winner to truly be random.

While I use raffle baskets all the time for all kinds of situations, I do want to share the advice of Lynn Huber. She runs raffles in a completely different way from myself. As you read through her advice, know that her product line requires more education than most (essential oils) and that everyone who enters her raffle is a winner.

- *I strongly suggest that you DO NOT use your own product for several reasons. One, as wonderful as your product is, it may not appeal to everyone. Two, many times if people enter a drawing for your product, they will not make a purchase because they want to wait and see if they've won. Instead, I have a prize such as a Kindle, Nook, or tablet. Many of these can be purchased for less than $100 and are great at capturing people's attention in a crowded event.*

- *Ask for all the information you need to properly follow up, then add a caveat if they fail to do so. Add in warnings such as, "All information must be completed to win!" or "If your phone or email are not legible, we can't contact you if you win."*

- *On the raffle tickets, I print "I'm interested in learning more about..." with several options for them to choose from such as: "How to use your product," "Making money while I stay at home with my kids," "Finding* solutions for my family," or "I just want to enter the draw." I add the last one in case they're not interested, so I don't waste my time with follow up.

- I make sure to have 5-6 clipboards preloaded with raffle cards so I always have enough in case things get busy.

- To encourage people to enter, I ask them if they'd like to enter to win a tablet and then add, "Someone has to win, it might as well be you!"

- If possible, try to label each entry as hot, cold, or warm before placing them in the basket.

- After the event, I follow up with everyone, but first with the "hot" leads. 99% of time you get voice mail. I leave a message that simply says, "Hi____. This is ____ from ____. You came by our booth this weekend and entered our draw. You are a winner. Call me at ____." 99% of them will call you back.

- While only one of them can win the tablet, other prizes you can offer include: "Night of pampering for you and three of your friends" or "customized makeover for you and three of your friends" or even a full-sized product. Pick prizes that fit what you have to offer.

- I let them know they can pick up their prize at one of my upcoming classes (that I already have scheduled). If they cannot make it to a class but seem really interested, I offer to meet them one-on-one. If they don't seem very interested, I let them know they will receive updates on upcoming classes and can redeem their prize at any one of those.

TABLES AND BOOTHS: WORKING THE EVENT

Prep time for the event is more than how long it takes for you to set up your table; keep in mind the delay factor in ordering products and having them arrive. Sometimes it can take up to a week to get banners or other signage from the printers, depending on how busy they are or if it's being shipped to you. I always encourage people to load their cars the night before. Make sure you arrive with plenty of time to unload, find parking, and get all of your materials to the event. Depending on the size of the event, you could require several trips to get everything to your space. Most specialists agree it only takes 30-60 minutes to set up the table or booth. That's standard for a one or two day event. The longer the event, the more trips and more time it takes to set things up.

If you are working a multiple day event, keep in mind you will need others there to help out. Seriously, at some point during an 8-hour event, you'll need to eat a meal or at least use the restroom. On top of that, working large events can be emotionally exhausting. It's tough work to maintain a high level of excitement for each person passing by. The specialists have a few bits of advice:

Susan Zabel:
I always make sure there are at least two of us at any event. One person can be there to just process sales and money. The other person is then available to talk to people, help with sales, and even recruiting. While family can help, it's even better to ask team members to help. When they do, I let them pass out their brochures with their names on it. It builds their confidence, knowledge, and experience to talk to so many people in such a short time frame. I do make sure they switch spots (talking to people and handling cash) so each gets a chance to build their own business.

Thomas Schrom:
When doing an event with over 50 confirmed guests, always try to bring a team member or friend. Things can get very busy. If you have more than one table, you want to able to keep an eye on everything. Make sure everyone that stops by to visit your location is treated friendly and no one is ignored.

This entire chapter has been about temporary retail locations held at events. All involve a bit of setting up, tearing down, and starting all over. Maybe you'd like to have the same kind of set up – but have it mobile. Quite a few direct sales representatives sell out of their own cars or even vehicles just for this purpose. Read on for more information.

STORES ON WHEELS

❖

This chapter is essentially about creating your own event with a mobile location – your car! I did this quite a bit early on to find customers and grow my team. I continue to do it even today while helping others on my team build their teams. Many of the same rules and efforts apply as mentioned in the last the chapter. To avoid repeating a great deal of information, I'm going to ask you to read that first (even if you jumped right to this chapter). While there is a great deal in common with working a booth at an event, there are differences.

TAILGATING

Where would you tailgate? Well, in my area, there are several informal "tailgate garage sales." Somehow a group of them decided to get together in the same location at the same days/times each week. People are selling homemade goods, direct sales goods, and second-hand garage sale type items. Many times, they create a Facebook group that vendors and customers alike join. Venders let people know if they will be there and what they are bringing along. Many times, orders from one week are then available for pick up the next week. In my experience, most of them set up in parking lots of businesses that have gone out of business. Of course, I strongly encourage you to check into your area's ordinances and abide by the law.

Some businesses welcome tailgaters. You just have to ask permission. Many times, they require that your set up is only for informational purposes – team building or sampling. I can't say for the entire nation, but in my area Big Lots stores will allow you to set up as long as you are not selling, have prior permission, and are professional in your conduct. It never hurts to bring in samples or full-size products to share with the manager and staff on hand for goodwill. There have been times I've asked for permission from mom and pop shops. They don't seem to mind. If all of my attention-getting efforts bring people closer to their store, then it's a win-win.

Aside from who owns the parking lot you park in, there are things to look for when deciding where in that parking lot to plant yourself. Make sure there is clear visibility from the road; the closer you set up to the road, the better. The exception to this is when you have permission from the business to be there. In that case, you want to be somewhere near the entrance so that customers don't have to walk far to get to you. If people are getting to you by car, make sure they have a place to park (so your presence doesn't cause a traffic jam or car accident). If people are getting to you by foot, don't make them walk far.

I look for heavier traffic areas in general. By that, I don't mean five-lane highways. I'm just saying, not the end-of-the-line back road that only has six cars drive by a day. You want a fair number of cars passing by on a regular basis. Also, it's handy to be near a stop sign or stop light. Why? People regularly have to slow down or stop for traffic flow. If everyone is speeding by at 35 MPH or more, they may be going so fast, they miss the chance to stop in even once they notice you're there. Make sure people have a couple of different ways to get into the parking lot – regardless of which side of the road they are driving on.

I'll be honest, I can take an hour or longer scoping out an area that is good for tailgating. Sometimes great spots pop right out at you. Other times you know it's a good area, but the exact right location doesn't present itself. Be prepared to set up, realize you picked a bad spot, and pack up and move two stores over to be where the traffic is. Once you find great locations, then you can always go back. It's just the initial work that takes time.

When tailgating, it's essential that everything fits in your car. This seems obvious, but I just wanted to point that out before you leave to start buying materials. Now, some people will literally sell out of their trunk. Others will set up a table just outside their car. Fold-in-half tables are easy to find at your local discount store. Table cloths make the set up look more professional, but clips to keep it from blowing away are essential. If you started the chapter here, please go back and read from the beginning. You'll learn a great deal about wind and how it affects setting up outside! Pop-up tents can be great, provided you have a way to keep them grounded. I have used heavy, fancy pop-up tents before, but it seems the more gear and parts involved, the easier they break. By the last time I used mine, MacGyver would have been proud of my paperclip and bubble gum efforts to keep it open and upright.

Now that you've found the perfect spot and set up, how do you get people to stop and check you out? Well, some people have great car wraps that draw attention. In fact, my friends Milagros and Carlos Garcia have what they call the "Magic Bus." It's a van that's completely wrapped with advertising. They also fitted it with an awning. Whether they have an event to attend or they set up in a random location, they just pack, pull out the awning for shade, and set up their table and such. It's a sight to see and really draws people over. Some people buy pop-up tents with the advertising printed there. A big tent with your company's name could be enough to draw people to you.

I prefer the method of making a sign from poster board and having someone stand near the street with the sign. Yes, that's right, just like high school students promoting a car wash. Many times, the person on the street is what draws people's eyes to the parking lot in the first place. When doing this, you need at least two people; one person waves the sign, one person works with people who come up to the table. Should the table get tons of people standing around, the person at the street usually needs to come over to help out. But, someone needs to go out to the street before they all leave. There is something about it, when you have people at your table, more people stop by. When no one is at your table, it's difficult to get someone to stop.

Other than choosing a great place to park and somehow drawing people's attention to your set up, tailgating is a lot like having an event. Read the chapter from the beginning if you have not yet. Everything else you need to know about tailgating will be found there.

STORE IN A TRAILER

I'm about to share information on having an entire store on wheels. This bit of info rides the rails between this chapter and the next. While it is a permanent personal store, its location varies day by day. This is a selling method perfected by Bell and Julio Hernandez of California. A great deal of this section will be information that they have graciously shared.

Bell and Julio actually bought a van, set a store up inside, and drive it around as a mobile store. They attached a ramp to the back so people can just walk right in to shop. This kind of set up didn't come easy – nor cheap. To give people an idea of what it takes, they shared their start-up costs:

- $8,000 – trailer

- $3,600 – professional car wrap of advertising

- $2,000 – for shelving units from IKEA (installed by Julio)

- $10,000 – inventory (housed both in the van and backup at home)

- Untold – buckets to organize inventory, all the little things needed to make it work

They like to take the van to events, flea markets, local parks, and even local gas stations. When looking for a spot, they make sure there is actual foot traffic. They make sure stores are close by or schools close by when school is about to let out. Because they are bilingual, they also look for Hispanic shopping areas.

Their goal is to park at about 10 spots a week with 2-3 hours at each location. If the traffic is slow, they pick up and move to the next spot. Some locations are repeat spots. They show up at the same location at the same time every week, almost like the mobile food trucks do. While many times, they pick up new customers, they do have regulars. Many times, they let customers know where they are by posting on Facebook.

Even so, they often get calls from regulars, asking where they will be next so they can go shopping.

The best times they have found on weekdays is 10am-1pm. Kids are in school and moms have more time to shop. For weekdays, they have sales goals of around $200. For weekends, especially when they are at a big event or a flea market (once a month), they have sales of $600-$1,400 a day, depending on the event. When working a bigger event, they make sure they have team members with them to help with the team building aspect. If you remember, Bell and Julio are also featured in the chapter on helpers, so that's a big part of their business as well.

As for inventory, they currently use the eyeball method. They have plans to develop a spreadsheet when they expand. However, for now, they can tell by looking at the shelves and the backup containers they have at home about what they need to buy every couple of weeks to keep enough stock on hand. They carry the most popular product lines from their company with just a few testers for people to try. While most customers pay in cash, they do use the Square for credit/debit cards and occasionally take checks, but only from those they know well. Clean up is done when they get home. Everything is restocked and put back in order so when it's time to leave the next day, they can hitch up and go.

They have some great tips to share with people considering this selling method:

- Always have a smile on your face.

- Be confident. If you don't know the answer, let the customer know you will found it out.

- Always be covered in company swag – hat, shirt, buttons, apron – whatever it takes so there is no question who you represent.

- If an area seems to have slow traffic or people seem shy to approach you, be prepared to venture out. Grab a couple of your company's brochures and a tester or two and start walking up to people. Smile. Be friendly. Many times, people will end up shopping or placing orders.

- Partner with your up-line (the people who signed you up) and those in your area. Our company has "district sales managers" who are there to help people in their assigned zip codes. We make friends with all of them so when we land in their area, we have their full support.

- Unless you have prior permission to park there, work from the assumption you will get kicked out. This actually helps assuage fears. If you assume it's going to happen, then it's not scary or sad when it does.

I want to end the chapter with a funny story they had to share. It shows just how unpredictable this sales method can be.

We stopped by a local fast food restaurant to get lunch. While eating lunch, we went ahead and set up in the parking lot. After a short bit, one of the employees came out and started running towards us. We figured we were about to get kicked out. Instead, he came up to us breathless, needing to buy something before we left! You just never know how you will be received.

This entire chapter has been about temporary retail locations – from a vehicle. Even though a great deal of the materials can usually be left in the car, there is still a fair amount of upkeep and transporting products and supports. Maybe you'd like to have a retail location, but not have to haul things around. One option is to set up a mini store inside your own home. Read on for more information.

STORE IN YOUR HOME

❖

Always wanted to own your own store, but put off by the large expense of time and money to make it happen? Like the idea of selling at events, but dread the set-up and tear-down? You're in luck! Many direct sales representatives across the nation have found the perfect middle ground – setting up a mini store inside their own home.

The great advantages to this method include a one-time set up. You have a quick commute to the office. You're already paying rent or mortgage on the space. It's a fabulous option for people with mobility issues and those needing to care for small children or a family member. As Kathy Dilley puts it:

> *I used to do a lot of outside events, but it took a lot out of me. Once I started having health challenges, I stuck with only having "my home" events.*

Of course, it's even more important at this point to check with your local HOA, city ordinances, and your insurance agent. At this point, you're operating a business in a residential area. I also encourage you to check with your tax professional (or at least get one). There may be tax benefits to what you're doing – depending on how you go about doing it.

Before you get started, take the time to envision how this will work for you, for your home, and for your family. Are you able to take over an entire room in the house to contain the store? Perhaps you have a garage sale on a regular basis. Are you drop-in-any-time or just set hours on certain days? There are many decisions to make as you set it up. As always, keep in mind your resources at hand: money, space, time, and abilities.

Everyone's in-home store will look different. Whereas Kathy Dilley holds garage sales every 2-3 weeks, both Adrienne Patrick and Sarah

Buckley redid entire rooms inside their homes. Sarah Buckley took over a spare bedroom to hold her inventory as well as serve as a photo studio for her online boutique. Adrienne Patrick created an entire boutique in order to do makeovers, host parties, and have product on hand to sell. She has great advice when building out your space:

Do not over spend on your space. Yes, it is a business investment, but is also takes away from your profit – profit meant to help your family.

There are generic items that many of you might need to purchase to set up your in-home store.

- Table and chairs for consultations
- Bookcases to act as product shelving
- Bins to hold bunches of the same product
- Banner or stand-up banner to set the mood of the room
- Product display stands, acrylics
- Brochures, order forms, pens
- Shopping bags
- Cash register, the Square, company-sponsored credit card processor, money bag/box, or some way to handle the money
- Money on hand to act as change for those paying in cash

Depending on your company's product line, you may need to buy specialized supports.

- Clothing racks, hangers, and mannequins
- Makeover stations
- Ring sizers, necklace sizers
- Bottles of water to mix your drink powder

- May need to designate a sink for customer use or have plenty of wipes on hand

Of course, anyone opening a store inside their home needs to have product on hand. This will look different for everyone depending on your company and your clientele. Each specialist interviewed handled inventory a different way:

Kathy Dilley
I keep the basics on hand. I buy them when they're on a great sale. I then price them a little higher than the sale I got. This allows my customers to get a good deal, but for me to increase my profit margin. I generally keep the same kinds of things on hand, but exactly what depends on my company's sales.

Adrienne Patrick
I keep 2-3 of high-frequency items on hand. As I sell items, I add them to a "saved" order with my company. Once I'm low on enough items, I will place one big order to bring my stock back to full.

Sarah Buckley
My company only makes 1,000 pieces in any one print. When people see an item they want, they need to buy right away because they'll probably never see it again. My inventory is always changing.

Deciding what to carry on hand is just part of your inventory decisions. Will you carry testers? If so, how many? Will you have an impulse purchase basket of low-cost items to add onto their purchase? Will you have a clearance section of items your company has discontinued and you can't return? What will be your return policy? How will you track what people buy (if you even want to)? How do you handle orders for things you don't carry on hand (shipped to them, they pick up, you deliver)? These are starter questions to ask yourself to make sure you've covered all the bases.

Of course, all that inventory needs to be sold for a price. If your company has stable pricing, you will probably keep the same price on your products. However, keep shipping costs in mind. For instance, if you buy inventory in bulk and notice that you pay about $2 in shipping for each large tub of protein powder, it is fair and wise to add a $2 shipping charge to the sale price. Anyone knows that if you bought one tub of protein powder by itself, you could end up paying $5-7 in shipping for that one item. Because you are buying in bulk, they are getting a discount anyway. Every company I'm aware of charges you sales tax at the time of purchase, so be sure to pass that cost along to your customers.

Some of you may be with companies that have regular sales. Others might be with companies that regularly discontinue items, but make it difficult for you to return them. In that case, you'll probably end up selling some items at a discount. Kathy Dilley's customers are used to buying at a discount, but she makes sure they know just how much they are saving.

I make big signs that say, "Regular Price (with tax): $x.xx Today Only: $x.xx" That way they know what a great deal they're getting.

While none of the specialists interviewed mentioned using helpers, you may consider how those in your home could help out. If you have a land-line phone, you may need to teach your children proper phone etiquette – or tell them to never answer "that" phone. You could have your children help keep the room clean as part of supporting the family or as a way to earn chore money. Spouses could be enlisted to hold down your store hours when you're called away for some reason. Make sure helpers know how to handle the money and complete a sale in general. Perhaps make sure they can contact you with questions or they know where to get answers if you're not available. Just because a store is inside our home does not mean the full responsibility needs to be on us alone.

Of course, we all know how ridiculous the saying is, "If you build it, they will come." Or at least I hope you all know how unrealistic that is. You need to let people know you exist! Everyone does this in their own way.

Kathy Dilley
I send out a blanket email to all of my regulars. I also put a sign out on the street to let people driving by know I have my company's products on hand for sale.

Adrienne Patrick
While I basically have a retail store in my home, I don't advertise it directly. When people come over for consultations or parties, they see that it's there. After that, they know they can always get more without the wait of an order. When I do outside events, I mention I have product on hand at home to build their confidence in working with me.

Sarah Buckley
I have a Facebook VIP group where I set up events for my Open Houses for my in-home boutique. I also have a Google+ business page that lists my address and such.

Of course, once people know you have a retail location in your home, you need to set boundaries. No one needs people showing up on family movie night or early in the morning before you've had your coffee. Unlike all the other methods of selling mentioned so far – the customer always knows how to find you. Everyone deals with this in different ways.

Kathy Dilley
Starting about late March (depending on the weather), I hold sales every 2-3 weeks. I do this on Saturday only from 9am-3pm. People in the area have become very loyal to my sales. I'll sell $600-700 each time.

Adrienne Patrick
People are able to shop by appointment only. The trick is to double and triple book your appointments to have a full room and not have to work multiple nights. Of course, the fun part of having the space in my home is when I do have to work evenings, my daughters always peak in and say goodnight in their jammies.

Sarah Buckley
I do have set hours, but most people set up an appointment to come by and shop.

Whatever you do, understand you are running a business. You made the decision to run it out of your home. Be sure to treat it as a store and those coming in as customers. One of my friends told me a tale of arriving at one such home. She came on time, but the lady wasn't ready to receive her. In fact, her hair was up in a towel from getting out of the shower. She asked my friend to wait 15 more minutes so she could get herself ready. The lady then turned to her husband and told him to stay in the room to "Keep an eye on her." Needless to say, my friend did not stay and the lady did not get a sale that day. If you're going to put a store in your home, be prepared to act like you have a store in your home.

Sometimes, after working lots of events, or tailgating, or even setting up a mini-store in their home, people decide they want to go big-time and open an actual retail store. Out of all the ways to sell, this requires the biggest commitment of all of your resources. Before moving on to the next chapter, double-check with your company's policies to see if you can sell in a retail location. Many do not allow it, but some do. For more information, read on.

YOUR OWN STORE

Owning a retail store is a bit like being a superhero; with great power comes great responsibility. There can be great rewards, but not without great risks. Yes, I do own two direct sales retail locations. My stores are actually licensed by my company (like a franchise, but fewer rules and no fees to pay). However, my company has not allowed new stores to open since 2010. I have checked with many, many other companies. None I have seen allow owning a store solely to sell their products. A handful of "Policy & Procedure" manuals I've seen have a provision where their line can be sold inside an existing location.

Please check with your company first to see if this option is possible. This is definitely not a gray area where you can" do first," but ask for permission later. I personally know someone who tried to open a quasi-retail location without prior permission. They were out $10,000 in investment when they were forced to close. I know of other heartbreaking stories like that.

Because of the limited availability of this option, and because of the huge consequences if people were to break the rules, I am keeping this chapter short. I will go over the basics and things to think about. My plan is to eventually write an entire book (along with video series) on how to own and operate a successful mom and pop shop. Truly, this method of selling deserves its own book, not just as a chapter inside another.

Many things are true for owning a store as they are for starting a direct sales business. It's just that the questions and answers are more important – if only because they require so much more of your resources. In case it's slipped your mind, resources include your money and your time, as well as your effort. In the case of opening and operating a store, there is a heavy load on your emotional energy and family support.

Things to have in place before considering opening a store:

- Ability to ask for help when needed

- Retail experience

- Product and industry knowledge

- Support Staff

  o Relationship with banker

  o Bookkeeper and/or CPA

  o Lawyer, or know where to find one

  o Commercial real estate agent

  o SBA Consultant or some sort of business mentor

- Start with the end in mind

That last bullet point refers to the need for you to know what you're about to create before you take the first step. If you have a solid foundation for what you're getting into, the actual creation of the store will go smoother than if you try to figure it out along the way. With that in mind, there are a few questions to ask yourself to make sure you head into the project in the right frame of mind.

- What do you want the store to provide for you?

- How much money are you willing to invest?

- What's your cut-off point for spending?

- When do you close the doors, rather than add more debt?

- How much time are you willing to invest?

- What will you do if/when the time required to stay open becomes overwhelming?

- How much are you willing to pour into learning?

- Is this for me?

Once you have honestly answered these questions and discussed the impact of owning a store with your family, you are ready to brainstorm how to create your store. There are steps you can follow to make the creation as smooth as possible.

Step 1: Create the vision for your store

Is your store posh and high-end? Will you be an outlet spot of old and discontinued products? Will half of your reason for existing be to build and train a team? This foundational decision affects many other factors.

Step 2: Location

Where is the best neighborhood for your vision to come true? Can you afford the rent?

Step 3: Pricing

Based on your vision and location, you'll decide on pricing. Will you have constant low prices, mixed pricing, full pricing, or premium pricing (higher than your company sells to cover shipping costs and such).

Step 4: Employees

Will it be just you? Will you have family help out? What is your dress code, training, and pay – just to name a few things to think about.

Step 5: Layout, fixtures, and displays

If you do not have experience in this area, you might search out a local college to see if students would be willing to mock up a layout on the cheap. Even a sophomore student will have a better eye than you if you've never done this before. Remember to buy display materials that match your pricing and vision. Don't forget sales tags and signage. Remember, your layout is the second-best defense against theft (with greeting people right away being the most effective deterrent).

Step 6: Sales equipment and software

This includes software to manage inventory and sales. You need some kind of register, whether it's a Point Of Sale system, a regular cash register, or an I Pad with a Square attached.

Step 7: Set an open date and work back from there

Ready, set, GO! Well, not just yet. You need to decide your opening date. From there, you can plan out your activities needed to lead up to that special day. Many things you need to do will overlap. On any given day, you might be placing your opening order, painting a wall before attaching a fixture, and approving an ad in the local paper.

With my first store, I fumbled with this so terribly I took nearly two months to open and I was a hot mess for at least a month after that. With my second store, I knew what I was doing and opened exactly 23 days from the first day they handed me the keys.

Once you've been open a few days, remember to take a deep breath. Know it's perfectly normal at this point to second guess what you've gotten yourself into. Many (most) new store owners cry themselves to sleep at some point in the first week – even the guys. I know that seems like an odd thing to bring up, but once you open your own store, me saying that will bring you comfort – if only so you know you're not alone.

I once heard that luck is basically a combination of opportunity and preparation. Hopefully this book has given you the tools and the maps necessary to move your business forward and help you build the life of your dreams. Best of "luck" to you!

PULLING IT ALL TOGETHER

$$\diamond$$

B elieve it or not, many people start a business with the words, "Wouldn't it be fun to…?" with no clue what they are getting themselves into.

I once met a couple of ladies who had recently opened a children's gym. Those kinds of places were the new trend at the time. With their combined 14 years of experience in physical education for young children, they thought it would be a great venture to start. What they didn't realize is that experience in working with children does not necessarily translate into an ability to operate a business. While chatting with them, it didn't take long to figure out they hadn't thought it through before getting started. When I asked a few questions about their situation, I got the response I thought I would. They felt they'd done well to come up with the down payment for the lease on their gym location. They were shocked when a mere 30 days later, the landlord wanted another payment. For goodness sakes! They had just opened their doors. How could the landlord expect more money so soon?

Please, take more time to plan out your business than these two ladies did. It could mean the difference between achieving your goals or not. If you're not sure exactly what you want out of your business, go back and read the first chapter. You'll find important questions that will help you design your business to help you achieve your dreams. I promise you'll be happy you did.

APPENDIX:
LEADERSHIP & TEAM BUILDING

— ❖ —

I know. I know. Just because you like to sell to people, doesn't necessarily mean you like to help sign people up to sell as well. I'm very aware of this. Now, some of you are super excited about team building and/or already have a thriving team that grows every day.

However, some of you get hives at the thought of training someone else to run their own business. But really, as you go about your life selling here and there, you are bound to run into others who would like to do what you do. If you don't sign them up to join your team, you don't end up keeping them as a customer. You not only lose them as a customer, but also as a team member.

Nearly all direct sales companies compensate their sales force for building teams. It's really just money left on the table if you don't participate in team building. Think of it this way, starting a business is just another product you can sell to your customers.

Of course, this is a book on sales, not team building. However, I would be remiss if I didn't share resources you could use to help learn more about the team-building process. As with any other sales method, the first place to turn to learn how to build a team is your company training and the person who helped you get started. Just as each company has a different product line, each company has a different take on how to build teams. Each company has a different team framework and compensation plan. Start there.

Next, there are a lot of great company-neutral resources that can help you learn about team-building in general.

Tom "Big Al" Schreiter:

- www.fortunenow.com

- He has written over a dozen books on network marketing and team building.

- He holds workshops in the US, Canada, and around the world.

- I have heard of him a great deal, but never read any of his books.

Eric Worre:

- networkmarketingpro.com

- Known best for his book and events: "Go Pro"

- He has other books, videos, and events and offers coaching and speaking.

- I have read his Go Pro book and know of many people who look forward to his big yearly event.

Robert Bliss Brooke:

- blissbusiness.com

- Known for his books, "The Four Year Career" and "Mach II with Your Hair on Fire"

- Offers coaching and multiple events and retreats a year.

- I have read both of those books and attended some of his training. Robert knows his stuff.

DSWA – Direct Selling Women's Association:

- dswa.org

- They sell books, offer coaching, and have many events.

- I have been certified in leadership by them through my company.

- Grace and Nicki Keohohou are great ladies with a heart-felt desire to help others. I have attended live training by both of them.

Verbal Aikido for Ultimate Networking Success

- https://igniteyourfreedom.leadpages.co/mastering-communication-grow/

- $50 discount for my readers if you use the link above ($248, reg. $298)

- 7+ hours of video training put together by James MacNeil, along with David & Tammy Stanely

- The program is a combination of communication, coaching, and presentations skills.

- I have taken the full Verbal Aikido training. I loved it so much I became a licensed partner in Verbal Aikido itself. This particular training is focused on those in direct sales and network marketing.

More about Verbal Aikido for Ultimate Networking Success in the words of David and Tammy Stanley:

David and I struggled with prospecting and approaching people for the business. Why were people not embracing the opportunity we shared? After a long process of discovery, we realized it was how we were delivering the message. It wasn't that they were unwilling to listen, but in how we communicated.

Regardless if you are just starting out or have been in the profession for a number of years, we're confident that you'll agree that communication plays a key role in your success. Of course, you need to fully engage in your company's offered training and follow their system. But, to further increase your success, it's important to increase your ability to communicate openly, honestly, directly, and respectfully.

Verbal Aikido is one such training. This is a life-transforming, one-of-a-kind, advanced communications skills philosophy and experientially delivered program that uniquely links emotional intelligence with the powerful non-adversarial philosophy of the Japanese martial art, Aikido.

Our online home study course has been built especially for people in the Network Marketing profession. The main focus is on communications training. However, there are bonus modules: Power Presenter, Million Dollar Speaker, and Pure Coaching, providing a well-rounded course that will, once you put it into action, skyrocket you and your business.

To recap this very short chapter: inviting someone to join your team to start their own business is just another item in your company's product line. To start, turn to your company's training and those who helped you start your business. Once you have that down, you would most likely benefit from further learning from one or more company-neutral trainers. Best of luck in this area of your business.

APPENDIX: SALES EXPERTS PROFILES

❖

Did you connect with a specialist's story? Do you want to find out more about them and what they do to excel in direct sales? Find them below! Everyone is listed in alphabetical order according to last names.

Debra Allen

- Company: doTERRA since 2013 (10 years in direct sales)

- Hometown: Liberty, MO

- Direct Sales Website: www.mydoterra.com/debraallen

- Social Media Links:

  o Facebook Profile: www.facebook.com/TheDebraAllen

  o Facebook Group: www.facebook.com/debforessentialoils

  o Twitter: @headbonbonbabe

  o Linked In: www.linkedin.com/in/myrepdeb

  o Pinterest: www.pinterest.com/myrepdeb

- About: In doTERRA, I am a Wellness Advocate at the level of Executive.

Jeanpeirre Bongiovi

- Company: Avon since 2011 (but helped mom for 23 years)

- Hometown: Glendale in Queens, NY

- Direct Sales Website: www.youravon.com/gbongiovi

- Social Media Links:

  o Facebook Profile: www.facebook.com/jeanpierrebongiovi

  o Facebook Page: www.facebook.com/Jeanpierres-Enchanted-Beauty-Parlor-422163237877740

  o Instagram: @AvonDude

  o YouTube: www.youtube.com/channel/UC2RHtJO9Sds46OkugfJRu4g

- About: I helped my mother with her Avon business for 23 years before starting out on my own. I sell at President's Council level and am a Gold Leader in Avon. I am a makeup artist and use my skills in my store, Jeanpierre's Enchanted Beauty Parlor.

Sarah Buckley

- Company: LuLaRoe since 2015 (3 years in direct sales)

- Hometown: Kansas City metro, MO

- Direct Sales Website: www.facebook.com/groups/lularoesarahandlaura

- Social Media Links:

    o Facebook Profile: www.facebook.com/lularoesarahbuckley

    o Facebook Group: www.facebook.com/groups/lularoesarahandlaura

    o Twitter: www.twitter.com/LuLaRoeSarah

    o Linked In: www.linkedin.com/in/sarah-buckley-104515

    o Instagram: @lularoesarahbuckley

    o Google+: http://bit.ly/1SDK2Hw

- About: I have been in the direct sales field for over three years. I also run a successful Avon business as a Silver Ambassador and I sell at President's Club level. I was awarded the Spirit of Avon in 2014, "because of an attitude of giving, sharing, and selflessness." I am married to my soul mate and have two wonderful step-daughters. I also have two lovable fur babies that make our family complete. I suffer from a chronic illness so LuLaRoe has been an answer to my prayers. It gives me purpose while allowing me to work at my own pace and still be successful.

Tracy Carden-Mason

- Company: Avon since 2008

- Hometown: Elyria, Ohio

- Direct Sales Website: www.youravon.com/TLCARDEN

- Social Media Links:

  o Facebook Profile: https://www.facebook.com/tracycardenmasonindependentavonrep

  o Facebook Group: https://www.facebook.com/groups/avonsteamspirit/

  o Facebook Group: https://www.facebook.com/groups/AvonBasketCases/

  o Twitter: https://twitter.com/ladyt702002

  o LinkedIn: https: https://www.linkedin.com/in/tracy-carden-mason-12656030

  o Instagram: https://www.instagram.com/_avonlady/

  o You Tube: https://www.youtube.com/results?search_query=Tracy+Carden-Mason

  o Pinterest: https://www.pinterest.com/ladyt70/

- About: I have been a single mom for five of my seven and a half years as an Avon representative. I have been with my fiancé Royal for two years and he helps me tremendously with my children; but, also my Avon business. I have eight beautiful daughters, a grandson, and a granddaughter, and he has a son, and a granddaughter. So, we now have a very large and wonderful family. Without them, I wouldn't be able to accomplish everything that I do. They are my motivation. I am a Silver Ambassador and President's Club member.

Arlene Cathey

- Company: Tupperware since 1995

- Hometown: Mound City, KS

- Direct Sales Website: www.mytupperware2.com/arlenecathey

- Facebook Profile: www.facebook.com/arlene.cathey

- About: Tupperware has been a help to my family and I for over 20 years. I have a grown son in Peru who is getting married.

Mary Cavanaugh

- Company: Coseva since 2014 (7 years in direct sales)

- Hometown: Orlando, FL

- Blog Website: www.thebookongreatness.com

- Social Media Links:

  o   Facebook Profile: www.facebook.com/mary.cavanaugh.52

  o   Twitter: @max4metals

  o   Linked In: www.linkedin.com/in/mary-pulles-cavanaugh-1a26a61b

- About: Mary is the mother of three beautiful daughters. Her youngest daughter suffered a vaccine-induced brain injury at age two and was later diagnosed on the autism spectrum. This diagnosis led Mary to search for treatment which in turn led her to the world of network marketing in 2009. She became an Autism Entrepreneur and is always looking for products that can lead to the recovery of Autism. Mary is a contributor to two books in the Thinking Parent Series, "From Hope to Healing: How Thinking Parents are Recovering Their Children and Uncovering the Truth" and "Autism and Puberty." Mary just finished her own book, "The Book of Greatness: How to Keep Shining Your Light."

Alice Chisholm

- Company: Avon since 2011

- Hometown: Aloha, Oregon

- Direct Sales Website: www.youravon.com/aliceChisholm

- Blog Website: www.pressonwithalice.com

- Social Media Links:

  o Facebook Profile: www.facebook.com/pressonwithalice

  o Twitter: www.twitter.com/pressonwithalice

  o Linked In: www.linkedin/in/alice-Chisholm

  o Instagram: www.instagram.com/pressonwithalice

  o YouTube: www.youtube.com/becomeavon

  o Pinterest: www.pinterest.com/aliceChisholm1

- About: Selling Avon absolutely thrills me. I sell at Rose Circle level and my team puts me at the level of Leader. My husband Tom and I have two sons, Zack and Alex. I'm one of nine children, and enjoy family gatherings. I was a middle school health teacher for 32 years. I believe in leaving a situation better than I found it.

Kathy Dilley

- Company: Avon since 1986

- Hometown: Liberty, MO

- Direct Sales Website: www.youravon.com/kdilley

- Facebook Profile: www.facebook.com/kathy.m.dilley

- About: I am a Leader and in the Honor Society for sales. I am #1 in team sales in my district.

Rhonda Dingman

- Company: Avon since 2012

- Hometown: Decatur, IL

- Direct Sales Website: www.youravon.com/rdingman

- Social Media Links:

    o Facebook Profile: www.facebook.com/rhonda.dingman.5

    o Facebook Group: www.facebook.com/Everything-Avon-by-Rhonda-482988125082606

    o Twitter: www.twitter.com/AvonLady001

    o Instagram: www.instagram.com/_youravonlady_

- About: In Avon, I am a Star Promoter and in the President's Club for sales.

Ginny Fiscella

- Company: Silpada Designs Jewelry since 2000

- Hometown: Overland Park, KS

- Direct Sales Website: www.silpada.com – search for rep Ginny Fiscella

- Blog Website: www.isellsilver.com

- Social Media Links:

  o Facebook Profile: www.facebook.com/savvysilvergirl

  o Twitter: www.twitter.com/savvysilvergirl

  o Linked In: www.linkedin.com/in/ginny-fiscella-87a38429

  o Instagram: www.instagram.com/silpada_savvysilvergirl

- About: I started with Silpada in 1999. I have earned every award Silpada offers. I say this not to brag, but to assure you that if you join my team, you are working with someone who has the knowledge and ability to help you be successful. I was the first Silpada representative to earn the title of Sterling Director. This is the highest rank obtainable with Silpada. I currently lead the number one sales team in Silpada with over $8,000,000 in annual sales. I'm consistently in Silpada's top 20 in personal sales (out of 20,000), including one year as the top sales person. I train representatives at Silpada's Leadership and National conferences, including keynote addresses to over 4,000 representatives. Nobody has developed more Silpada Leaders than me. I will help you be successful!

Susan Hamel

- Company: Avon since 2002 (36 years in direct sales)

- Hometown: Bedford, NH

- Direct Sales Website: www.youravon.com/shamel

- Social Media Links:

  o Facebook Profile: www.facebook.com/susan.hamel.14

  o Facebook Group: www.facebook.com/ groups/503515156475199/

  o Twitter: @AvonSusanNH

- About: Susan has been self-employed since 1988 when she started her own bookkeeping business. After working with two network marketing companies and a party plan, in 2002, Susan found her passion with Avon. She began recruiting right away and has moved up to the top level, Senior Executive Unit Leader. With representatives all over the country, her unit sales were close to $900,000 in 2015. She is a top recruiter and top sales representative in her district. Susan is also a Beauty Advisor and enjoys volunteering her makeover skills at a local fashion house. Susan has earned many trips during her career. She has traveled to Hawaii, London, China, the Caribbean, Key West, Puerto Rico, and Mexico, Nashville, Kansas City, Orlando, Connecticut, Chicago, Hollywood, and Las Vegas. Believing that life is about helping others, she has volunteered with the local women's shelter and Toys for Tots. Each year, she holds a Christmas party for the residents at the local women's shelter. Her passion is helping women improve their lives and attain their goals in life. "We all have dreams and goals. My job is to help make yours come true!" Work Until Your Dreams Come True!

Rhonda Henderson

- Company: Avon since 1997 (30 years in direct sales)

- Hometown: Grand Prairie, Texas

- Direct Sales Website: www.youravon.com/rhondahenderson

- Facebook Profile: www.facebook.com/rhonda.henderson.528

- About: I have been happily married to my husband Ricky for 27 years. I enjoy a little wind therapy while riding my Harley Davidson and traveling with friends. We enjoy spending time with our fur babies, Lexi and Bugsy. I worked several jobs before becoming an entrepreneur at age 21 and owning Nails by Rhonda. I received my Bachelor's Degree in Marketing from Dallas Baptist University in 1992. I then found my passion in direct sales. I was honored in NYC in 2007 with the Woman's Empowerment Crusader award for my $86,000 in fundraising efforts for the Avon Foundation through breast cancer walks. I was the 2008 recipient of Avon's Woman of Enterprise award, the highest achievement in Avon. Through my high volume of sales, I have earned many fabulous vacations and cruises to places such as the Bahamas, Las Vegas, Mexico, Alaska, and more. I sold at President's Council level for many years and am an Executive Unit Leader.

Bell & Julio Hernandez

- Company: Avon, since 2009

- Hometown: Newark, CA

- Direct Sales Website: www.youravon.com/bellhernandez

- Facebook Profile: www.facebook.com/BellHernandez

- About: My husband and I both work Avon fulltime. We love it because it gives us the opportunity to be with our kids. We do fundraisers to help with soccer, baseball teams, etc. We are Gold Leaders and in McConnell Club for sales, but we have goals to move higher.

Lisbeth House

- Company: Avon since 2005

- Hometown: Vancouver, WA

- Direct Sales Website: www.youravon.com/lisbethhouse

- Facebook Profile: www.facebook.com/lisbeth.house

- About: I have a husband and two of the best kids in the world, Andrew, 18 and Emily, 15. I am a Gold Ambassador in Leadership and in Honor's Society in sales.

Lynn Huber

- Company: doTERRA since 2015 (15 years in direct sales)

- Hometown: Salt Lake City, UT

- Direct Sales Website: www.MydoTERRA.com/LynnHuber

- Blog Website: www.LynnHuber.com

- Social Media Links:

  o Facebook Profile: www.facebook.com/lynnjhuber

  o Twitter: www.twitter.com/lynn_huber

  o Linked In: www.linkedin.com/in/lynnhuber

  o Instagram: www.instagram.com/lynnjhuber

  o YouTube: www.youtube.com/user/lynnjhuber

  o Pinterest: www.pinterest.com/lynnjhuber

- About: Fifteen years ago, Richard and I entered Network Marketing. He has been my partner from the beginning. We started out slowly, selling to friends at events and on my email lists. But then we tried passing out brochures around the neighborhood. Within 16 months, we had enough to pay cash for a brand new Honda CRV. That was a huge wakeup call for us. Wow! What else could we do if we tried? Well, I gave up my corporate job eight years ago and have never looked back. We built up a $1.9 million business from home. We are debt-free - no house payment, no credit card debt. We have both the financial and time freedom to do the things we want. The best part about our business is how many lives we have been able to help change through our business. After you're making enough to live on, it becomes about so much more than the money – and that's where we're really blessed.

Suzy Ishmael

- Company: Avon since 2007

- Hometown: Staten Island, NY

- Direct Sales Website: www.youravon.com/si

- Book: co-author - A View From the Top: Volume 3: http://www.amazon.com/dp/098971294X/ref=cm_sw_r_fa_dp_RldTwb0KDCSPB

- Social Media Links:

  o Facebook Profile: www.facebook.com/suzy.ishmael

  o Store Facebook Page: www.facebook.com/theavonshop

  o Twitter: www.twitter.com/avonbigapple

  o LinkedIn: www.linkedin/in/suzyishmael

  o Instagram: www.instagra.com/theavonshop

  o Pinterest: www.pinterest.com/theavonshop

- About: Suzy Ishmael currently lives on Staten Island, NY with her husband and two children, Saleem and Sarah. She was born in Trinidad & Tobago, majored in Business Studies, and started working in the oil industry at the age of 18. In 2000, she got married and moved to the USA. In 2001, she started working for not-for-profit agency that provides services for the developmentally disabled. Motivated by the desire to be debt free, and finding that her full-time job was not fulfilling her financial obligations, she began selling Avon in 2007 while still working full-time. She graduated from AUL Academy and advanced to Executive Unit Leader with a team that has earned over $1,000,000 in unit sales. She has achieved President's Council level with over $112,000 in personal sales, making her

#1 for Top Seller and Leadership titles in her district. In 2011, Suzy opened a Licensed Avon Beauty Center (LABC) serving the New York area. Through her high volume of sales and leadership skills, Suzy was able to pay off her mortgage in 10 years and buy their second dream home 6 months later. Her skills in direct marketing have earned several all-expense paid trips for her and her family to Hawaii, Hollywood, Orlando, and Vegas to name a few. Her goal is to retire from her full-time position and let her Avon business supplement that income. Suzy's passion is sharing the Avon opportunity and helping empower women to make their dreams come true.

Dr. Paul Jernigan

- Company: Life Matters since 2015, 8 years in direct sales

- Hometown: Overland Park, KS

- Direct Sales Website: www.lifematters.net/feelalive

- Business Website: www.lifeflowkc.com

- Social Media Links:

  o Facebook Profile: www.facebook.com/drpauljernigan

  o Facebook Group: www.facebook.com/groups/lifemattersmidwest

  o Twitter: www.twitter.com/DrPaulJernigan

  o Linked In: www.linkedin.com/in/drpauljernigan

  o SlideShare: www.slideshare.net/DrPaulJernigan

  o Periscope: @drpaulj

  o Instagram: www.instagram.com/drpauljernigan

  o YouTube: www.youtube.com/c/pauljernigan

  o Pinterest: www.pinterest.com/drpauljernigan

- About: I was an eye doctor and at the age of 32, despite tremendous success in my profession, I realized I wanted to impact humanity in a deeper way. I just couldn't imagine sitting in that room doing the same thing for the next 40 years like all my colleagues. I was grateful for my profession... but like anything else...I listened to my gut...and I'm so glad I did. About that time, Network Marketing came into my life. My initial resistance to the idea, driven by my ego and fear, quickly left when I fell in love with a product. This began a short journey of 10 months to retirement from when I started seriously working my NWM business on a very part-time basis. The organizations and teams I've developed and have been blessed to be a leading part in the last 8 years, and have moved and average of $1.5 million dollars of product annually. I have personally enrolled only 40 people over my short 8 year career in NWM. I'm now 40 and couldn't be happier that I have been able to not continue to build in this industry, and have the freedom that allowed me to open an Alternative Healing Practice in Overland Park, KS. This is just another way I get to give back to humanity on Spiritual, Physical, Mental and consciousness planes. My partner and I continue to give back, doing things that we are passionate about and we look forward to continuing to connect with amazing people. We love to build teams that help us grow...both professionally and personally. Humanity is a mirror for us if we allow it to be; if we can step back and witness how we relate to what we are seeing. We move through life with hearts full of gratitude. Our Alternative Healing practice can be found online at www. lifeflowconnections.com.

Adrienne Patrick

- Company: Mary Kay since 2005

- Hometown: Kansas City metro, Missouri

- Direct Sales Website: www.marykay.com/apatrick26

- Facebook Profile: www.facebook.com/adrienne.patrick.37

- About: My husband, Travis, and I have been married for 11 years. We have two kids who are five and three. Our adopted dog is named Petey. We go to a church that we love. I'm able to serve as the team leader of the 3-5 year old kids' church team. I also serve in the three year old room. I volunteer at our local animal shelter. I have great friends!

Theresa Paul

- Company: Avon since 1994

- Hometown: Florida, NY

- Direct Sales Website: www.youravon.com/tpaul

- Blog Website: www.theresapaul.com

- Social Media Links:

  o Facebook Profile: www.facebook.com/theresa.a.paul

  o Facebook Group: www.facebook.com/groups/tuesdays.with.theresa

  o YouTube: www.youtube.com/user/Theresa54345

- Weekly Call: Tuesdays at 8pm EST – see Facebook group for details

- About: Born in southern California, Theresa moved to New York on her 21st birthday to be with the man she loved. 30 some years, and 3 wonderful sons later, she is still in NY and still married to the love of her life. Theresa began her Avon business in 1994, quitting her job in the schools several years later to work her Avon business full time. It only took a few years for her to reach President's Council as a National Top Seller and then on to become a Senior Executive Unit Leader with more than 900 members currently on her team. She has earned many trips and awards for her personal sales as well as for her team's success. This has created great energy for Theresa and her ever-growing team, with whom she continues to work and share the skills she has acquired to help them create their own successful Avon business.

Thomas Schrom III

- Company: Avon since 2013

- Hometown: Rotterdam, NY

- Direct Sales Website: www.youravon.com/tschrom

- Blog Website: manofsuccessblog.wordpress.com

- Social Media Links:

  o Facebook Profile: www.facebook.com/thomas.schrom

  o Facebook Group: www.facebook.com/Schrom-Family-Avon-Independent-Sales-Rep-127660910742196

  o Twitter: www.twitter.com/miakrulz

  o Instagram: www.instagram.com/disney_and_avon

  o YouTube: www.youtube.com/channel/UCJQsAyGNc3Do1w8-0WLpWUw

- About: I am the eldest of seven children. Family is very important to me. I have two dogs that I love very much; a pug and a Maltese. My current leadership title with Avon is Gold Ambassador. I have sold at President's Club level all three years with Avon.

Lisa Scola

- Company: Avon since 2001

- Hometown: Youngstown, OH

- Direct Sales Website: www.youravon.com/avonlisas

- Blog Website: www.lisascola.com

- Social Media Links:

  o Facebook: www.facebook.com/avonlisascola

  o Facebook Group: www.facebook.com/groups/successwithscola/

  o Instagram: @avonlisas

  o YouTube: www.youtube.com/user/avonlisas

- About: Lisa Scola started selling Avon as a personal shopper in 2001, and turned that around after being with Avon for 2 years. Lisa has been in the President's Club or above every year she has been with Avon. She has 3 children and has enjoyed being a stay-at-home mom since she started. Although she didn't start this business as a single mom, after a divorce, she quickly learned that she could earn enough money with her business to still stay home and raise her children on her own! Lisa enjoys all that she has earned with her business; not just a substantial income but a bunch of free trips and extra bonuses as well! This business has changed her life. Be sure to check out her website at www.lisascola.com for even more information!

Emily Seagren

- Company: Avon since 2008, 10 years in direct sales

- Hometown: Rockford, IL

- Direct Sales Website: www.youravon.com/eseagren

- Blog Website: www.makeupmarketingonline.com

- Social Media Links:

    o Facebook Profile: www.facebook.com/emily.seagren

    o Facebook Group: www.facebook.com/groups/Makeup. Marketing.Online

    o Twitter: www.twitter.com/your_avon_rep1

    o Linked In: www.linkedin.com/in/eseagren

    o Instagram: www.instagram.com/avonrepemily

    o YouTube: www.youtube.com/avonrepemily

    o Pinterest: www.pinterest.com/avonrep2

- About: Emily Seagren has been an Avon representative since 2008. She sells at the President's Inner Circle Level (over $280,000 annually), owns a Licensed Avon Beauty Center, and is a Gold Leader with over 300 Avon Representative team members in 40 states nationwide. In 2015, Emily sold over $67,000 online and recruited 240 team members as a result of her online marketing efforts. In 2015, Emily was awarded the prestigious award of Avon Woman of Enterprise. Emily has earned all-expense paid trips to Hawaii, Punta Cana, Cancun, Puerto Rico, Hollywood, San Diego, Las Vegas, New York, Orlando, a cruise to the Bahamas, and a cruise to Alaska. In July 2014, Emily had brain surgery to remove a benign tumor. She was especially grateful for having built a big business that provides for her family when she cannot work.

Susan Zabel

- Company: Avon since 2002

- Hometown: Vancouver, WA

- Direct Sales Website: www.youravon.com/szabel

- Social Media Links:

  o Facebook Profile: www.facebook.com/susan.zabel.7

  o Twitter: www.twitter.com/suelovesavon

- About: All of my kids are grown up. I have two dogs, three cats, and two birds. I have been successful despite a struggle with dyslexia. My husband is a great help to me. I sell at the level of Honor's Society and am a Leader in Avon.

ABOUT THE AUTHOR

❖

Elizabeth Demas has been an entrepreneur for most of her life. The week she turned 18, Elizabeth joined direct sales with Avon. She started out walking door-to-door in her assigned territory. Over the last 20+ years, she has been in over a dozen different direct sales companies. This current 13-year stint with Avon is her fourth time selling Avon. She believes most direct sales companies are basically good to join. You just have to find the one right for you. Avon has worked really well for her.

She currently lives in the Kansas City area with her husband and children. Her oldest is living on his own. The second is back and forth from college. The two younger children live at home. Over a dozen foster children have lived in the home, but that chapter of life is just about to close. Inspired by her youngest child, Elizabeth is soon starting a foundation in her name. The Annabelle Foundation will help others affected by Down Syndrome, children exposed to drugs before birth, and special needs adoptions. More information can soon be found at: www.annabellefoundation.org.

This book represents a start to Elizabeth's commitment to helping others build their businesses. Visit www.SuccessWithElizabeth.com to find out about more business supports: an online business-growth support group, training video packages, ongoing webinars and more!

- Blog Website: www.SuccessWithElizabeth.com

- Store Website: www.kcmegastore.com

- Direct Sales Website: www.youravon.com/edemas

- Social Media Links:

  o Facebook Profile: www.facebook.com/elizabeth.demas

  o Facebook Group: www.facebook.com/groups/
    womenwithabusiness

  o Facebook Stores: www.facebook.com/AvonMegaStore

  o Twitter: www.twitter.com/elizabethdemas

  o Twitter Stores: www.twitter.com/AvonMegaStores

  o Linked In: www.linkedin.com/in/elizabethdemas

  o YouTube: www.youtube.com/user/elizabethdemas

  o Pinterest: www.pinterest.com/avonelizabeth

36318981R00106

Made in the USA
San Bernardino, CA
19 July 2016